Hills of the Severn Valley

A guide to the 60 best hills and walks to them in the Severn Valley

by

Barry Smith

Published by Where2walk

Hills of the Severn Valley

Copyright @ 2024 Barry Smith

The right of Barry Smith to be identified as the authors of the work has been asserted by them in accordance with the Copyright, Designs and Patents Act 1988.

All rights reserved. No part of this publication may be reproduced, stored in a retrieval system or transmitted in any form or by any means, electronic, mechanical, photocopying, recording or otherwise, without the prior permission of the authors.

ISBN: 978-0-9956735-7-1

Every reasonable effort has been made by the author to trace copyright holders of material in this book. Any errors or omissions should be notified in writing to the author, who will endeavour to rectify the situation for any future reprints.

Main Front Cover Photo: Millennium Hill:

Secondary Photos: Cam Peak and Broadway Tower

Designed and published by Where2walk

Printed by B & D Print Services

Contents

Worcestershire Beacon

About the Severn Valley 6
Selecting the Hills 7
Full List of Hills 8
How to Use this Book 12
Safety in the Mountains 13
Regional Breakdown ....
- Birmingham to Worcester 14
- The Malverns 36
- Gloucester & the Forest of Dean 52
- The Cotswolds 76

Hill Listings Explained 102
Relative Hills Society 102
Log of Walks 104
About the Author 110

Introduction

"Around the Severn Valley, between Birmingham and Bristol, lie many hills, some well-known like the Malvern Hills, some lesser known. This book is a guide to walks up the 60 best hills. Anyone completing them will appreciate that the area is one of the most beautiful in Britain."

The hills in this book lie between Birmingham and Bristol and most of them are found in the counties of Worcestershire and Gloucestershire. The M5 runs through the middle of both counties, connecting Birmingham and Bristol, and the distance between the two cities is just under 90 miles. There are many well-known towns in Worcestershire and Gloucestershire, including Worcester, Great Malvern, Broadway, Tewkesbury, Cheltenham, Gloucester, and Stroud.

The area includes some of the most beautiful parts of the Heart of England, including the Cotswolds, the Malvern Hills and the Forest of Dean.

The hills of the Severn Valley divide into four parts: Birmingham to Worcester (Worcestershire), the Malvern Hills (mainly in Worcestershire), the Forest of Dean (mainly in Gloucestershire), and the Cotswolds (Gloucestershire).

Looking north along the Malvern ridge

About the Walks

How were the walks selected?

To put together the list of the Hills of the Severn Valley, I started by looking at all the hills in the area with a 30m (just under 100ft) drop or prominence. There are over 100 of these.

I then discounted any hills that are on private land. Apart from the obvious difficulties of access, hills on private land tend not to be good hills. I also deleted poor hills; those hills that are close to the road and any hill under 75m or 250ft high which are too low.

To finalise the list, I climbed all the hills by alternative routes. The 60 hills selected are listed in full on pages 8 to 11.

The map below references the 4 main regions I used in order to simplify the area of the Severn Valley.

Cam Peak near Dursley

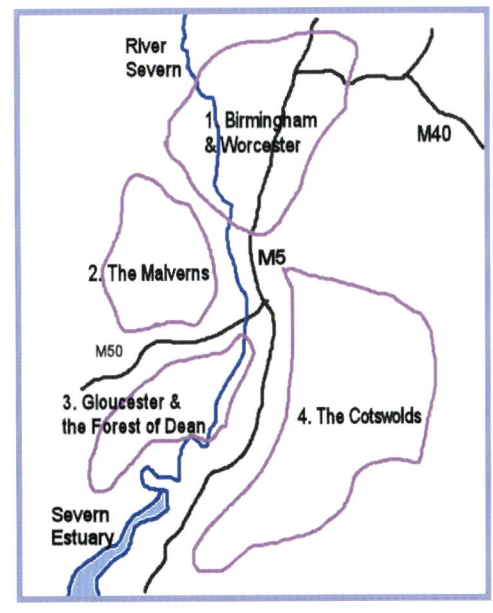

Listing of the Hills 1

Map Ref		Page No	Height (m)	Height (ft)
	BIRMINGHAM TO WORCESTER			
1	Frankley Beeches	16	256	840
2	Walton Hill	18	316	1,037
3	The Four Stones	18	309	1,014
4	Chapman's Hill	22	287	942
5	Beacon Hill	22	298	978
6	Rednal Hill	22	268	879
7	Abberley Hill	24	283	928
8	Woodbury Hill	24	275	904
9	Walsgrove Hill	24	265	869
10	Rodge Hill	24	188	617
11	Bredon Hill	28	299	981
12	Ankerdine Hill	32	149	489
13	Piper's Hill	33	120	393
14	Elbury Hill	34	98	320
	THE MALVERNS			
15	Worcester Beacon	38	425	1,394
16	North Hill	38	397	1,302
17	Pinnacle Hill	42	357	1,117
18	Herefordshire Beacon	42	338	1,109
19	Swinyard Hill	44	272	892
20	Midsummer Hill	44	284	932
21	Ragged Stone Hill	46	254	833
22	Chase End Hill	46	191	627
23	Howler's Heath	48	182	597
24	Suckley Hills	50	170	558
25	Suckley Hills West Top	50	164	537

Regional Maps 1

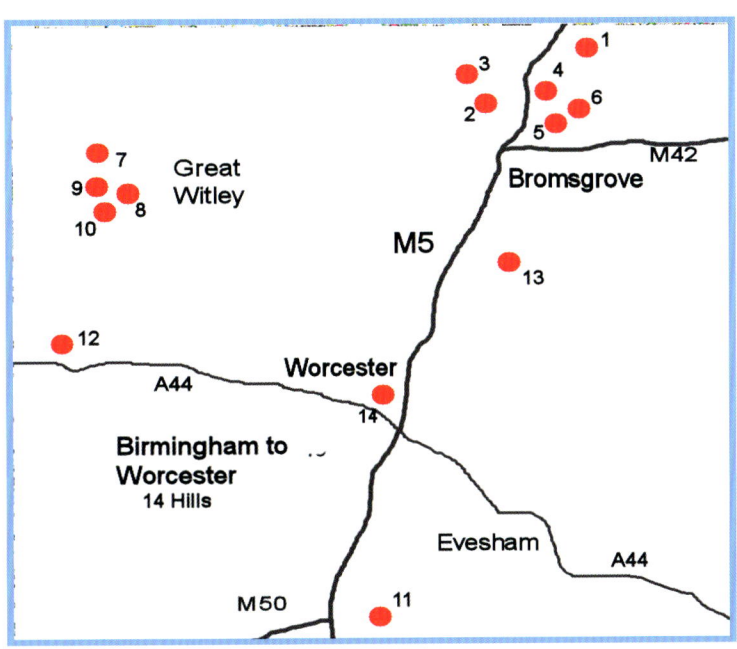

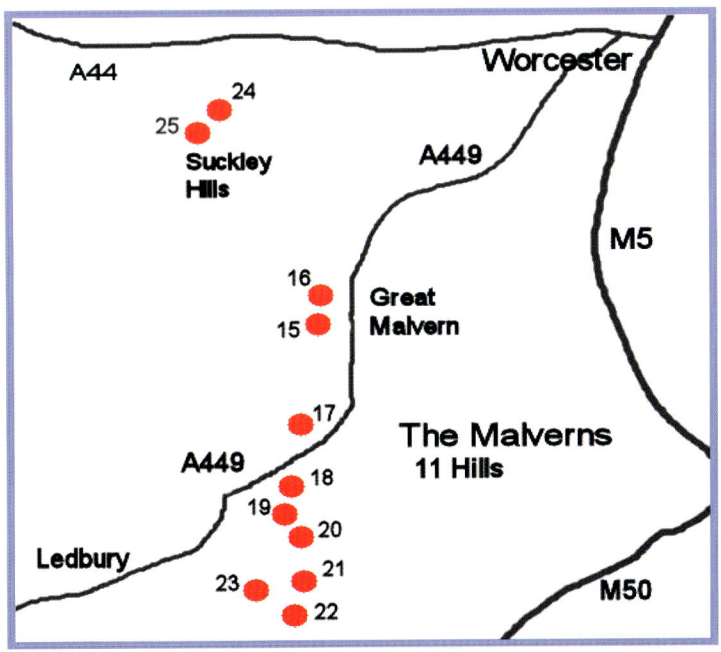

Listing of the Hills 2

Map Ref		Page No.	Height (m)	Height (ft)
	GLOUCESTER & THE FOREST OF DEAN			
26	May Hill	54	296	972
27	Huntley Hill	54	202	663
28	Wigpool Common	56	279	915
29	Chase Wood Hill	57	203	666
30	Edge Hill	58	281	920
31	Chestnuts Hill	58	196	643
32	Hangman's Hill	58	180	591
33	Staple Edge Hill	60	228	748
34	Blaze Bailey	62	208	682
35	Crabtree Hill	64	203	666
36	Serridge Inclosure	64	207	679
37	Little Doward	66	222	730
38	Coppet Hill	66	201	659
39	Ruardean Hill	68	290	951
40	Buck Stone	70	280	917
41	Blake's Wood	70	243	797
42	Sandhurst Hill	72	88	288
43	Churchdown Hill	73	155	509
44	Robins Wood Hill	74	198	650
	COTSWOLDS			
45	Seven Wells Hill	78	319	1,047
46	Shenbarrow Hill	78	304	997
47	Nut Hill	81	119	390
48	Swell Hill	82	235	771
49	Cleeve Hill	84	330	1,083
50	Leckhampton Hill	86	293	961
51	Birdlip Hill	88	300	983
52	Crickley Hill	88	273	896
53	Painswick Beacon	90	283	928
54	Minchinhampton Common	91	207	679
55	Doverow Hill	92	143	469
56	Crawley Hill	93	251	824
57	Cam Peak	96	184	602
58	Cam Long Down	96	220	722
59	Downham Hill	96	199	653
60	Stinchcombe Hill	99	219	718

Regional Maps 2

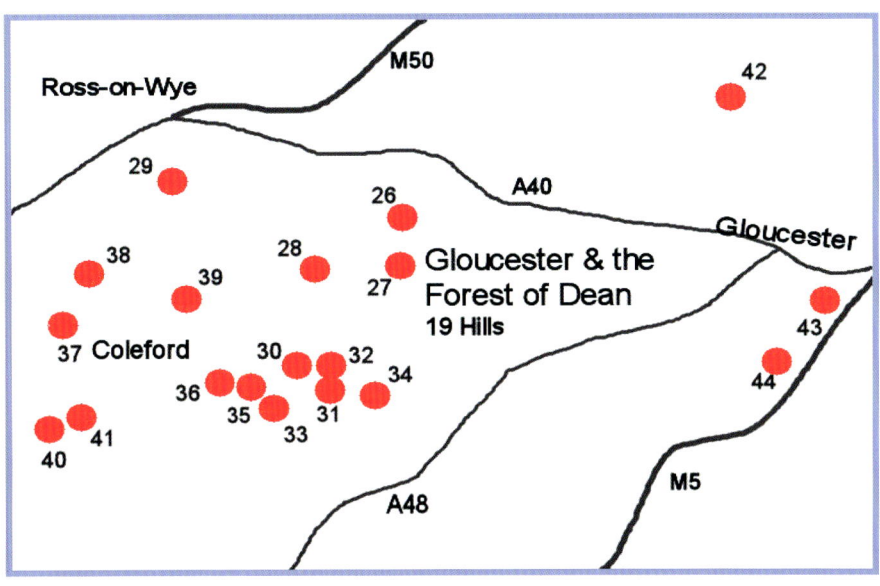

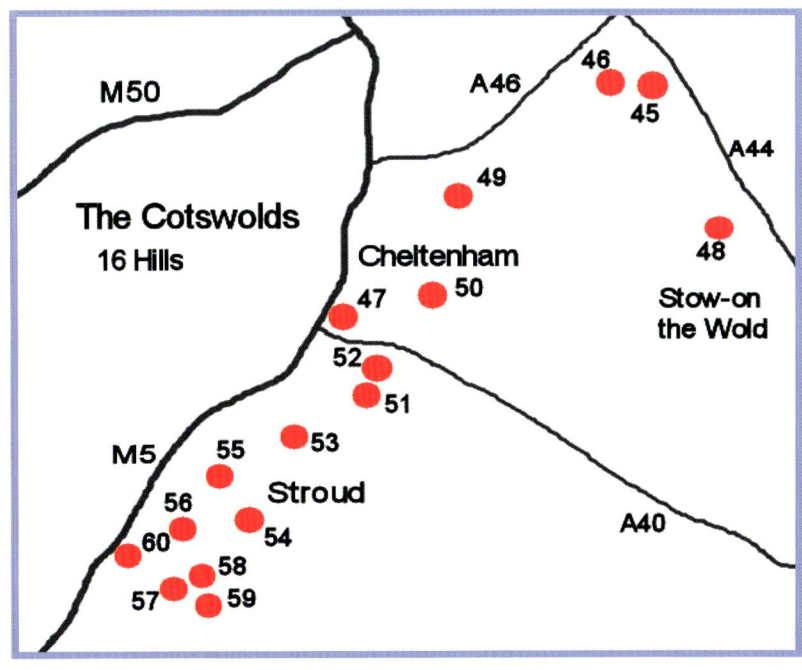

About the Book

Layout of the Book

The hills are divided into four regions;

1 Birmingham to Worcester, excluding the Malvern Hills. This section includes the Clent and Lickey Hills, some great hills near Abberley, and the Bredon Hill.

2 The Malvern Hills and nearby Suckley Hills. These are mainly in Worcestershire, but include one hill in Gloucestershire and two hills in Herefordshire.

3 The Forest of Dean and hills in west Gloucestershire. These include three hills in Herefordshire.

4 The Cotswolds as they run north to south from Broadway to Dursley.

The hills are divided into walks, in total 40 walks cover the 60 hills. Between one and four pages are devoted to each walk. There is a full description of the walk, photos of places on the walk, details of parking and postcodes where possible, and the distance and difficulty of each walk.

I have graded the walks 1 to 4;

1 is a relatively easy walk, probably taking less than an hour and mainly on good paths.

2 is a moderate walk, may take up to 3 hours, but not too strenuous.

3 is a longer walk and/or on more difficult terrain.

4 is for the longest and most strenuous walks, these may take 4 to 5 hours to complete.

Liability

All information in this book is given in good faith and no liability is accepted in respect of any damage, loss or injury which might result in acting on it.

Naming the Hills...the TomDous

I intend to refer to these hills as the **TomDous** in memory of my father and Uncle, Tom and Douglas, who introduced me, my brothers and my cousins to hill walking. Most of our hill walking was in the Lake District with visits to all the major peaks including Scafell Pike, Scafell, Helvellyn and Great Gable, when staying in Grasmere in 1963 and 1964. However, Douglas and his family lived in Cheltenham and we used to visit them regularly. I remember trips to the Malverns and the Forest of Dean, including one in particular to the Worcestershire Beacon in 1967. Ever since, I have looked forward to visiting the Malverns and managed to do so regularly

Safety & Access on the Walks

Safety on the Walks

This book is only intended to be a broad guide to the routes up the best hills in Worcestershire and Gloucestershire. The O/S Explorer Maps OL14 (Forest of Dean), OL45 (Cotswolds), 167, 168 (Stroud), 179 (Gloucester and Cheltenham), 190 (Great Malvern), 204 (Worcester) and 219 (Wolverhampton) would be helpful to plan the route together with a compass. A GPS can be used as an aid to a map and compass but not as a replacement. Mobile phones can also help but they are easily damaged, run out of battery and it is not always possible to get a signal.

The Hill Bagging website provides further information and logs on each hill. Put in the name of the hill then hill bagging to access this information.

Appropriate clothing should be worn and, if walking on your own, a second person informed of your route and likely return time. In groups always plan for the slowest member of the party. These precautions should help reduce any dangers and make the walks more enjoyable.

Access

The hills in this list are all on Access Land or with a Right of Way running close to the summit at the time of going to print. Where there is a Right of Way or a concessionary path going over private land, please stay on the path. Access land is shown on the O/S Explorer Maps by yellow shading.

Please follow the **Countryside Code.** The rules are as follows:

1. You should use public rights of way, for example footpaths or bridleways.
2. Use gates, stiles or gaps in field boundaries if you can. Climbing over gates, walls, or fences can damage them.
3. Leave gates as you find them or follow instructions on signs.
4. Leave farm animals alone. Don't interfere with animals if you think they are in distress, try to alert the farmer instead.
5. When you take your dog out, always ensure it does not disturb wildlife, farm animals or other people. Dogs must be kept on a lead at all times when near livestock.
6. Do not block gateways, driveways or other paths with your vehicle.
7. Follow paths unless wider access is available, such as open country or registered common land.
8. When driving, slow down or stop for horses, walkers and farm animals, and give them plenty of room.

Birmingham to Worcester

This area includes the Clent and Lickey Hills ten miles south-west and south of Birmingham, the Abberley Hills near Great Witley, Bredon Hill and two smaller, isolated summits, Pipers Hill to the east of Droitwich Spa, and Elbury Hill, the high point of Worcester. There are 14 hills in this section including well-known names such as Abberley Hill, Bredon Hill and The Four Stones.

On the Lickey Hills

Frankley Beeches

Visit this lovely woodland summit close to Birmingham.

About Frankley Beeches

Frankley Beeches is the most northerly hill on the list and lies only a few miles from Birmingham city centre.

Height	256m/840ft
Summit GR:	SO 992797
Map:	O/S Explorer 219
Hill Category:	Tump

Frankley Beeches

Frankley Beeches is a small clump of trees, standing prominently on a hilltop. The beeches are a legacy of the Cadbury family and are now owned by the National Trust. The Beech trees are tall and attractive, see picture opposite.

Walk Summary

Whilst it is possible to park in a lay-by close to the summit, it is preferable to start from the 15th Century church near Frankley Reservoir, where it is usually possible to park.

Walk Description

Start from next to the church and follow the Right of Way past a house and along an avenue of trees. Take care crossing a stile (it appears in need of repair) and ascend along a field edge. Now cross a road which may be busy and go straight into a copse of trees, Frankley Beeches. Walk to the far end of the copse to see the views. The Trig Point is on the outside of the copse on the south-west side. It is accessed by a small path.

Distance:	2.5km/1.5 miles
Height to Climb:	70m/250ft
Start:	SO 999804
Difficulty:	1

Birmingham to Worcester

Summit copse of Frankley Beeches

Clent Hills

Great views and historical sites on this walk over the Clent hill summits.

About Walton Hill
Walton Hill is the highest point of the Clent Hills. There is a Trig Point and good views from the summit.

Height	316m/1,037ft
Summit GR:	SO 943798
Map:	O/S Explorer 219
Hill Category:	Marilyn

Walk Summary
The walk starts at the National Trust car park on the north-east side of the Clent Hills (charge). There is an open-air café next to the car park. The walk traverses the Four Stones ridge passing the high point and the Four Stones. The route descends to the valley, then climbs to the summit of Walton Hill. From Walton Hill, there is a straightforward descent and walk north back to the car park.

Distance:	4.5km/3 miles
Height to Climb:	200m/650ft
Start:	SO 938808
Difficulty:	3

About The Four Stones
This hill is named after the Four Stones on the western end of the ridge, where there is a viewfinder. However, the high point is 400 metres east.

Height	309m/1,014ft
Summit GR:	SO 937806
Map:	O/S Explorer 219
Hill Category:	Tump

The Four Stones
The Four Stones are passed on the walk, 400 metres east of the high point of the hill. They appear to be a Megalithic site from prehistory. However, the site was erected in 1763 by workers of the eccentric landowner, George Lord Lyttleton of Hagley Hall.

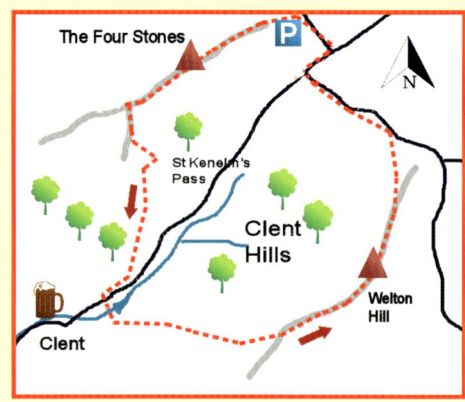

Birmingham to Worcester

Walk Description

Looking west from near Four Stones

The walk starts from the National Trust car park at the north end of the Clent Hills, a short distance south of the A456, between Halesowen to Hagley. There is a charge for using the car park (free for National Trust members) and refreshments are available.

Walk back to the minor road at the east end of the car park and turn right along the road. After 50 metres, turn right to follow a track up the hillside. This path follows the ridge of Four Stones Hill. It passes over the high point after approximately 400 metres, just before a gate at the end of the woodland.

Continue walking south-west on the path along the ridge of Four Stones Hill. After a few hundred metres, the Four Stones and the viewpoint are reached. There are good views west from here. Turn left to descend in a southerly direction, then turn right to continue to descend south. The path leads down to a minor road which goes through the middle of the Clent Hills, St Kenelm's Pass.

At the road, turn right, and after a short distance, a path goes off to the left. Follow this path for 100 metres and another minor road appears. Turn left then follow signs to Clent Hills and Walton Hill. A path climbs the hillside in an easterly direction. When the summit ridge is reached, turn left to follow the ridge to the Trig Point on the summit of Walton Hill.

Continue east along the path, then left at a fork in the path and descend north. The path descends to a minor road. Turn left to walk along the road to a T junction. Turn right at the T junction, then take the next left to return to the National Trust car park.

Heading up Four Stones Hill

Birmingham to Worcester

Viewfinder on the top of Beacon Hill!

Waseley & Lickey Hills

A beautiful walk partially in Country Parks, only a few miles from the centre of Birmingham.

About Chapman's Hill

Chapman's Hill is the high point of Waseley Country Park just east of the M5 south of Birmingham. It is a popular hill with a viewfinder at the summit.

Height	287m/942ft
Summit GR:	SO 972779
Map:	O/S Explorer 219
Hill Category:	Tump

About Beacon Hill

Beacon Hill is the highest summit in the Lickey Hills with a mock castle at the summit. It can be ascended from the car park to the south-west, but it is best climbed as part of a circuit of all three hills.

Height	298m/978ft
Summit GR:	SO 988760
Map:	O/S Explorer 219
Hill Category:	Tump

About Rednal Hill

Rednal is a pleasant hill on a wide ridge of trees. It is a neighbour of Beacon Hill.

Height	268m/879ft
Summit GR:	SO 997762
Map:	O/S Explorer 219
Hill Category:	Tump

Walk Summary

The walk starts at the north car park for Waseley Country Park and follows the North Worcestershire Way over Chapman's Hill and to the Lickey Hills Country Park. Turn left here to go over Beacon Hill, across the golf course on a Right of Way, and to the summit of Rednal Hill. The return route avoids the climb back over Beacon Hill.

Distance:	11km/7 miles
Height to Climb:	250m/800ft
Start:	SO 972782
Difficulty:	4

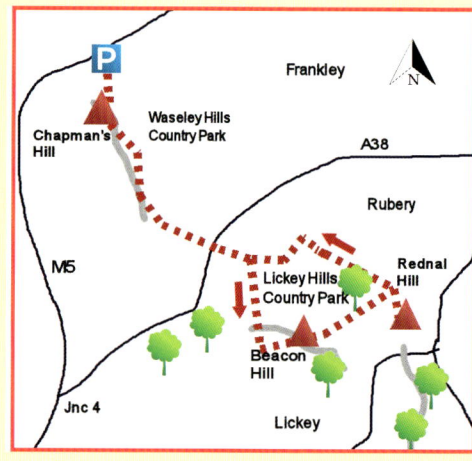

Birmingham to Worcester

Walk Description

This is an interesting walk on good paths with a short roadside section through a housing estate. The walk starts at the north car park at the Waseley Country Park. In 2023 there was a £3 charge to park all day. There is a café next to the car park.

Follow the North Worcestershire Way south-east up the hillside to the viewfinder at the summit of Chapman's Hill. Continue south-east and then south on the North Worcestershire Way. The path exits the Country Park and after nearly 2km reaches a minor road. Turn left and walk for about 50m, then right to cross a bridge over the A38. When the road bends left, continue straight ahead on the North Worcestershire Way.

Follow the path for a few hundred metres to another minor road. Turn right to follow the North Worcestershire Way up the hill, initially next to the road, then on a path through the woods. The path continues up the hill coming out of the trees at the Country Park. Look to the left and the castle obelisk can be seen. Turn left to walk to this, the summit of Beacon Hill.

Continue east on a path which skirts the left-hand side of the woods, passing a Trig Point. This path descends to Lickey Hills Golf Course and crosses the course. Take care to follow the Right of Way across the golf course. The path, now going north-east, leaves the golf course and goes straight up the hill immediately ahead.

On arriving at a ridge, turn right and follow the path up the hill for a further 200m to the unmarked summit of Rednal Hill.

Return along the path but continue straight ahead on the path to the housing estate below. Turn left and follow the road, which becomes Rednal Hill Lane, through the estate. Turn left at the end of the estate onto Beacon Hill Road and follow this 500m up the hill until the North Worcestershire Way goes off to the right. Follow the Way back to the start.

Lickey Hills Country Park

The Birmingham Society for the preservation of Open Spaces, which included several elders of the Cadbury family, purchased Lickey Hills Country Park in 1888 and built the castle structure with the view finder at the summit of Beacon Hill. Today the park has over 500,000 visitors per year.

Abberley Hill & Great Witley

An excellent walk traversing four hills and passing a number of historical sites.

About Abberley Hill
Abberley Hill is the highest hill in the area. It is a popular hill with a Trig point at the summit.

Height   283m/928ft
Summit GR: SO 752672
Map: O/S Explorer 204
Hill Category: Hump

About Rodge Hill
Rodge Hill is the most southerly of these four hills with a long north to south ridge.

Height   188m/617ft
Summit GR: SO 747624
Map: O/S Explorer 204
Hill Category: Tump

About Woodbury Hill
Woodbury Hill is an Old Iron Age Hill Fort, now wooded. A public footpath runs through the middle of the Iron Age Hill Fort although there is no public footpath to the high point.

Height   275m/904ft
Summit GR: SO 747645
Map: O/S Explorer 204
Hill Category: Tump

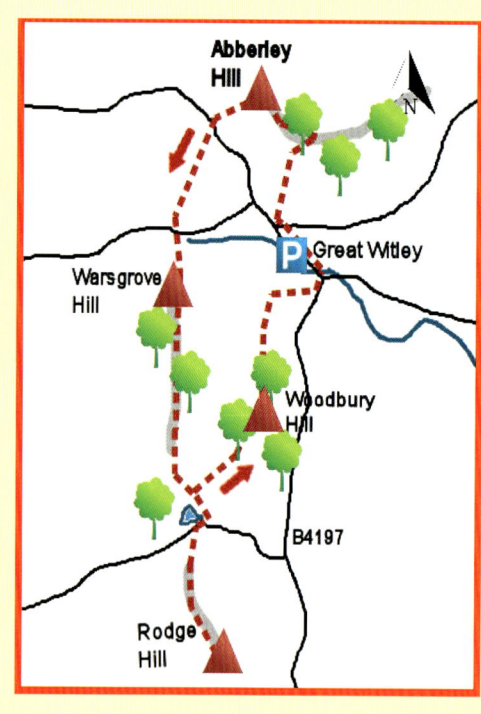

About Walsgrove Hill
Walsgrove Hill is a steep sided grassy hill with a pleasant ridge running north to south.

Height   265m/869ft
Summit GR: SO 743658
Map: O/S Explorer 204
Hill Category: Tump

Birmingham to Worcester

Abberley Hill from Walsgrove Hill

Walk Summary

This is a superb walk of approximately fifteen kilometres passing through woodland and historical features. The walk is nearly all on good paths with a couple of short road sections.

Distance:	15km/9 miles
Height to Climb:	460m/1,500ft
Start:	SO 755659
Difficulty:	4

The detailed walk description is on the following two pages.

History of Great Witley

The walk starts near the Parish Church of Great and Little Witley, which is famous for its jewel-like stained glass windows and paintings by Italian artists.

The walk passes Abberley Clock Tower, a prominent, distinctive clock tower built in 1883. It can be seen from six counties. It also goes through the middle of a large Iron Age hillfort at the top of Woodbury Hill.

In addition, it is a short trip to Witley Court with its magnificent Palladian palace destroyed by fire in 1937. However, the gardens have been restored to their former glory.

Abberley Hill & Great Witley

Walk Description

The walk starts from the large car park at the Village Hall at Great Witley. At the entrance to the car park turn right and follow the road to the junction with the A451. Continue for a short distance, then turn right to follow the path up the hill, signposted Abberley.

Continue just east of north. The path enters woodland, and at a junction, follow the right-hand path which makes its way east to join the ridge on which Abberley Hill is situated. On arriving at the ridge turn left along the Worcestershire Way and follow the ridge to the Trig Point denoting the summit of Abberley Hill.

Near the summit of Abberley Hill

Birmingham to Worcester

The Worcestershire Way is now followed for 6km over Walsgrove Hill to Rednal Hill at the south end of the walk.

Initially the path descends south-west to a minor road. Turn left along the road following the Worcestershire Way. The route crosses the road and continues south past the west side of Abberley Hall School and the Clock Tower.

Turn left at a road and, after a short distance, cross the road to join a minor road heading south. After walking 50m along this minor road, the Worcestershire Way goes steeply up the hill to the left. Follow this path to the summit of Walsgrove Hill. The high point is just north of the bench.

Follow the path south along the ridge. After one kilometre the path doubles back for a short distance, then continues south. A few hundred metres later the Worcestershire Way bends left, then continues south again. When the Worcestershire Way joins a road, follow the road south turning right at a T Junction just past a quarry. After 400m the Worcestershire Way leaves the road and heads south on a path which climbs to the summit of Rodge Hill. The summit is near a bench.

Return north to the road and follow the road until just past the quarry. Look for a footpath sign on the right. Follow the footpath north-east through two fields, and then through a wooded area (where the footpath can become overgrown in the summer). On exiting the wooded area, turn right, then left to climb to the edge of the Woodbury Hill Fort.

Shortly after this, tracks go off to both the left and right signposted 'no footpath'. The high point of Woodbury Hill is about 100 metres up the track to the left at a ruined stone structure, but this is private woodland.

Follow the footpath north through the woodland for a further kilometre. The path comes out at a road. Turn left along the road for a short distance, then there is a signpost on the right-hand side of the road to Great Witley. Follow this path which comes out just south of the village. Turn left along the road, then left again at the main road to return to the car park.

Bredon Hill

An ancient hill fort and 18th century Parson's Folly share the summit of this well-known and popular hill above the Vale of Evesham.

About Bredon Hill

Bredon Hill is a bulky hill positioned between the Malvern Hills and Broadway Tower. It has commanding views in all directions.

Height	299m/981ft
Summit GR:	SO 958403
Map:	O/S Explorer 190
Hill Category:	Tump

Walk Summary

There are numerous places from which to ascend Bredon Hill. The suggested walk commences at the village of Elmley Castle where there is parking and refreshments. This allows a circular route ascending north of Castle Hill and descending south of Castle Hill.

Another good start point is Woollas Hall Farm where there is a Vineyard (grid reference SO 945411). From here the Wychavon Way can be followed to the summit. This route is shorter (5km for the return journey).

Distance:	8km/5 miles
Height to Climb:	230m/800ft
Start:	SO 983411
Difficulty:	3

Parsons' Folly

At the summit, next to the Iron Age hill fort known as Kemerton Camp, is a small stone tower called Parsons' Folly.

The tower was built in the mid-18th century for John Parsons, Squire of Kemerton Court. It was intended as a summer house, with extensive views of the surrounding countryside.

The top of the tower is at 1,000ft

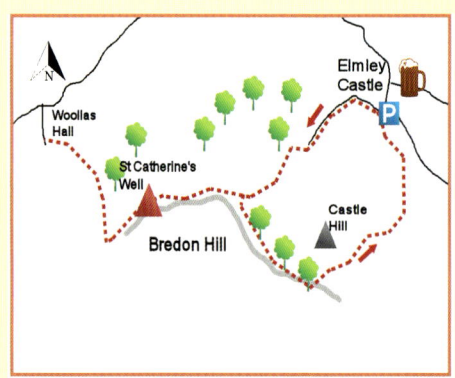

Birmingham to Worcester

Walk Description

The summit on Bredon Hill

The walk starts from the car park at the village of Elmley Castle. Walk to the centre of the village, then follow the minor road going north-west out of the village. The road makes a sharp left turn, then continues up the hill (Hill Lane). After 1km the minor road ends at Hill House Farm. Continue on a path up the hill, going left at a fork in the path.

Continue up the hill. The path reaches the summit plateau and continues west to the hill fort and folly at the summit. There are good views north and west.

Return on the same path for approximately 1km, then turn right to follow the Wychavon Way south then south-east just above the tree line. After another kilometre turn left along a right of way which runs south of Castle Hill. After following this track for 1.5km, go left at a fork to return to the car park at Elmley Castle.

Birmingham to Worcester

Kermerton Camp on Bredon Hill

Ankerdine Hill

A good summit for a picnic.

About Ankerdine Hill

Ankerdine Hill lies on the Worcestershire Way just north of the Suckley Hills. The summit is close to the car park, but the walk can be extended.

Height	149m/489ft
Summit GR:	SO 737565
Map:	O/S Explorer 204
Hill Category:	Tump

Walk Description

There is a small car park about 200m north of the summit. If driving west from Worcester, turn right off the A44 to Knightwick, follow the B4197 for 1km to the top of the hill where there is a sharp right turn to the car park. A track, the Worcestershire Way, is followed north for 200m to the summit and picnic table.

Ankerdine Hill

Piper's Hill

Walk in ancient woods near Droitwich Spa

About Piper's Hill

Piper's Hill is only marginally higher than the B road which runs through the woods and past the summit. However, the hill gives an excellent walk of under one hour around the ancient woods whilst ticking off the summit.

Height	120m/393ft
Summit GR:	SO 959650
Map:	O/S Explorer 204
Hill Category:	Tump

Walk Description

This walk of just over 1km starts from the car park off the B4091 at the north end of Piper's Hill. Cross the road and walk round the eastern perimeter of the woods initially.

The high point is just north of the house that you pass on the right-hand side. Continue round the woods. The path recrosses the road and follows the north, then west perimeter returning to the car park.

Car Park at Piper's Hill

Elbury Hill

A visit to the high point of Worcester City

About Elbury Hill

Elbury Hill is a short walk from Elbury Park Road, but I recommend adding Leopard's Hill close by which is only 10cm lower. The area containing Elbury Hill (sometimes known as Elbury Mount) and Gorse Hill is a local nature reserve. The summit area contains a Severn Trent reservoir.

Height	98m/320ft
Summit GR:	SO 869559
Map:	O/S Explorer 204
Hill Category:	Tump

Walk Description

There is roadside parking at the top of the hill on Elbury Park Road (Grid Reference SO871559). From here it is a short walk of a few hundred metres west on a tarmac track to the summit of Elbury Hill with its covered reservoir. After returning to Elbury Park Road, I suggest climbing Leopard's Hill which is only ten centimetres lower and appears to be the better hill.

To climb Leopard's Hill walk south down the hill to the B4637. Cross the road, turn left and follow a path towards the hill from next to the Texaco Garage. Continue on the path past two benches and through a gate. After going through the gate, the summit of Leopard's Hill is up the hill on the left.

The distance to climb both hills is approximately three kilometres.

Elbury Hill

In the past Elbury Hill was usually accepted as the most picturesque place in Worcester, believed to be a key place of worship at the time of the Druids.

However the hill was acquired by Worcester Corporation for a reservoir and today no traces of its more glamorous past exist.

Birmingham to Worcester

Summit of Elbury Hill

Elbury Hill from Leopard's Hill

Malvern Hills

The Malvern Hills are the best-known hills in Worcestershire. Two of the hills are in Herefordshire, The Herefordshire Beacon and Midsummer Hill. The lower Suckley Hills are also included in this section, as these are part of the Malvern Hills Area of Outstanding National Beauty.

There are eleven hills in this section including the highest hill in this book, the well-known and popular Worcester Beacon at a height of 425m (1,394ft).

The Malvern Hills

North Malvern Hills

Iconic, skyline walking over the most popular and highest hills in the area.

About Worcestershire Beacon

The Worcestershire Beacon is the County Top of Worcestershire. It is the highest hill in this book, and the best known. There is a Trig Point and Viewfinder at the summit.

Height	425m/1,394ft
Summit GR:	SO 769452
Map:	O/S Explorer 190
Hill Category:	Marilyn

Walk Summary

The walk starts at Upper Wyche. It goes over the summit of the Worcestershire Beacon and Sugar Loaf on the way to North Hill. It returns on paths bypassing the summits.

Distance:	6.5km/4 miles
Height to Climb:	300m/1,000ft
Start:	SO 769438
Difficulty:	3

About North Hill

North Hill is the second highest summit in the Malvern Hills. It lies at the northern end of the ridge and is seen as a twin of the Worcestershire Beacon.

Height	397m/1,302ft
Summit GR:	SO 769464
Map:	O/S Explorer 190
Hill Category:	Tump

Malvern Spring Water

The Malvern Hills are known for their spring water – initially from holy wells, and later the Spa town of Great Malvern. The production of modern bottled drinking water started here.

Malvern Hills

Walk Description

Summit Of Worcestershire Beacon

The walk starts at Upper Wyche where there is parking, a café and a pub. The parking gets very busy at weekends. An alternative is to walk up the Worcestershire Beacon from the centre of Great Malvern. This route is steeper with more ascent, but there are a multitude of paths to the summits of Worcestershire Beacon and North Hill from the town.

Starting from one of the car parks at Upper Wyche, follow the tarmac track north to a minor col between Summer Hill and Worcestershire Beacon. Continue north on the middle track which climbs the ridge to the summit of the Worcestershire Beacon.

The summit of the Worcestershire Beacon is a popular spot, particularly in summer. There is a Trig Point and viewpoint. This is the highest point in any direction for nearly 50 miles, so the views are expansive.

Descend north for 400 metres, then climb north-west to the summit of Sugar Loaf hill, a climb of just under 100ft. Sugar Loaf can be bypassed on the east side, but it is worth climbing this pleasant hill.

Descend north to the col below North Hill, turn right for a short distance, then climb north to the gap between Table Hill and North Hill. Turn right and climb to the summit of North Hill.

The route back to the car park follows broadly the same route as the outward journey, but both Sugar Loaf and the Worcestershire Beacon can be bypassed by paths on the east side.

Malvern Hills

Millennium Hill from Herefordshire Beacon

Central Malvern Hills

Complete Herefordshire Beacon and Pinnacle Hill in a two-legged walk from the British Camp car park.

About Pinnacle Hill

Pinnacle Hill is the high point of the next section of the Malvern Hills just to the south of the Worcestershire Beacon.

Height	357m/1,117ft
Summit GR:	SO 768421
Map:	O/S Explorer 190
Hill Category:	Tump

About Herefordshire Beacon

Herefordshire Beacon lies on the main chain of Malvern Hills and is just in Herefordshire. It is the first of five hills in the book which are in Herefordshire.

Height	338m/1,109ft
Summit GR:	SO 760400
Map:	O/S Explorer 190
Hill Category:	Hump

Medieval 'Ringwork'

The summit of Herefordshire Beacon is the site of a medieval 'ringwork', which is thought to have contained a timber structure with its own tiny bailey or yard. It may have been a hunting lodge, or a small castle built in connection with the boundary formed by the hills. It would have been a very distinctive landmark for miles around

Walk Summary

Park between the two hills at the British Camp car park. Walk south following a path which climbs the hillside and reaches the summit of Herefordshire Beacon in about 15 minutes. Continue south over Millennium Hill, descend south, then turn back north to return to the car park. Cross the road and continue the walk north to Pinnacle Hill.

Distance:	6km/4 miles
Height to Climb:	270m/900ft
Start:	SO 762403
Difficulty:	3

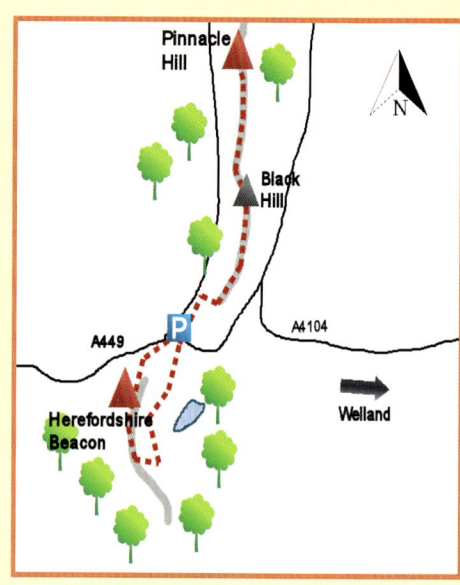

Malvern Hills

Walk Description

Looking north from Pinnacle Hill

This is a two-legged walk climbing Herefordshire Beacon and Millennium Hill initially, then returning to the start before climbing Pinnacle Hill. There is parking at British Camp car park (charge).

The path climbs Herefordshire Beacon from the west side of the car park. Keep right to follow a good path which climbs north-west directly to the unmarked summit of Herefordshire Beacon. Continue south for 400m to the bald summit of Millennium Hill (pps 40-41). Descend south-east to join the Three Choirs Way which is followed north back to the British Camp car park.

To climb Pinnacle Hill, continue north on the road which passes the left side of the Malvern Hills Hotel. Once past the hotel, a path goes up the hill to the right. Follow this, keeping to the left to reach the main ridge of the Malverns. Follow the ridge for 1.5km, walking over Black Hill and continue to the summit of Pinnacle Hill. To vary the return journey, follow the path on the west side which traverses below Black Hill to the Black Hill car park. A path beside the road is followed to British Camp car park.

Pinnacle Hill can also be climbed from the north starting from Upper Wyche (see Worcestershire Beacon walk) and walking over Perseverance Hill and Jubilee Hill.

Swinyard & Midsummer Hill

Two superb hills close to the centre of the Malverns give an interesting circular walk.

About Swinyard Hill

If walking south from Herefordshire Beacon, Swinyard Hill is the next recognised hill on the Malverns. There is a car park south of its summit.

Height	272m/892ft
Summit GR:	SO 762386
Map:	O/S Explorer 190
Hill Category:	Tump

About Midsummer Hill

Midsummer Hill stands at the top of a large Iron Age hillfort. The summit, just over the county border and therefore in Herefordshire, is one of the best summits in the Malverns.

Height	284m/932ft
Summit GR:	SO 760375
Map:	O/S Explorer 190
Hill Category:	Tump

4

Eastnor Obelisk

This very prominent 90ft high Obelisk, which dominates the west side of these hills, was put up in 1812, around the same time as Eastnor Castle was built. The monument is for distinguished members of the Somers Cocks family, who have plaques written on each side of the Obelisk.

Walk Summary

The walk starts from the Swinyard car park between the two hills. I suggest completing this walk anti-clockwise and climbing Swinyard Hill first. From Swinyard Hill the Three Choirs Way is followed south, with an optional excursion to the prominent Eastnor Obelisk. Finally Midsummer Hill is climbed before returning north to the car park.

Distance:	6km/4 miles (inc obelisk)
Height to Climb:	240m/800ft
Start:	SO 766381
Difficulty:	3

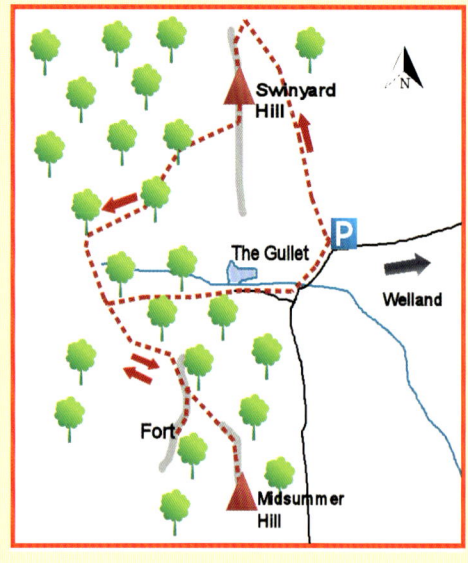

Malvern Hills

Walk Description

Coffin shelter at the top of Midsummer Hill

Start from the car park just west of Berrow Downs and walk north below the main Malvern ridge. After a kilometre the path climbs to the Malvern ridge. On reaching the ridge, turn south to follow the Three Choirs Way to the summit of Swinyard Hill. Continue south for a short distance, then follow the Three Choirs Way as it descends south west.

The Three Choirs Way leaves the access land and goes south-west through Gullet Wood. When it turns south the Eastnor Obelisk appears to the right. This can be visited by an optional detour.

The Three Choirs Way continues south-east, and after 300m, a path climbs up the hillside to the left and enters the ancient hill fort of Midsummer Hill. Climb to the summit of the hill with its coffin like shelter. Follow the outbound route back to the col between Midsummer Hill and Swinyard Hill. Turn right here to return to the car park.

Ragged Stone & Chase End Hill

Villages and hills combine to give a quintessential view of English country life.

About Ragged Stone Hill

Ragged Stone Hill is a fine hill situated south of the A438 road (Tewkesbury to Ledbury), and just within the county boundary of Worcestershire.

Height	254m/833ft
Summit GR:	SO 759364
Map:	O/S Explorer 190
Hill Category:	Tump

About Chase End Hill

Chase End Hill lies south of Ragged Stone Hill. There is a Trig Point at the summit.

Height	191m/627ft
Summit GR:	SO 761355
Map:	O/S Explorer 190
Hill Category:	Tump

Walk Summary

This is an excellent walk over two of the southerly summits of the Malvern Hills. The walk starts from the parking area on the north side of the A438 at Hollybush. It goes south over Ragged Stone Hill and Chase End Hill, then returns along the west side of Ragged Stone Hill.

Distance:	4km/2.5 miles
Height to Climb:	200m/650ft
Start:	SO 761369
Difficulty:	3

Curse of Ragged Stone Hill

As a punishment for breaking his vows a monk was made to crawl to the summit of Ragged Stone Hill daily. He cursed the mountain for all time for those who visit its slopes.

The monk however was only a character in the 19th century novel by Charles F Grindrod including all the best features of any novel: love, lost and the 'bad guys'.

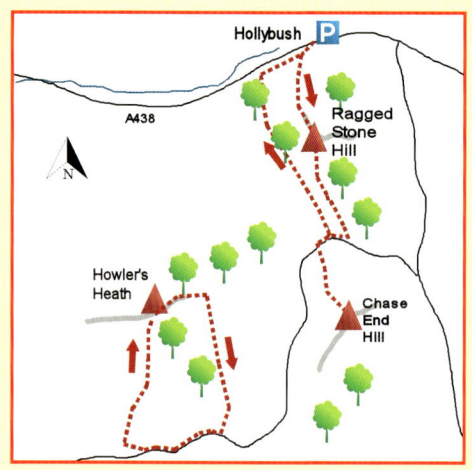

Malvern Hills

Walk Description

Ragged Stone Hill from Chase End Hill

There is a parking area just off the A438 at the top of the hill at Hollybush. The parking area is between Midsummer Hill to the north, and Ragged Stone Hill to the south.

Cross the road and walk 100m in a westerly direction to pick up a path which goes left up Ragged Stone Hill. Follow this south, taking the left-hand branch at a fork. The path climbs steeply up the hill to the magnificent summit and viewpoint of Ragged Stone Hill.

Continue south on a good path down the hill to the hamlet of Whiteleaved Oak, bearing left when arriving at a residential area. Shortly after the residential area, a minor road is reached. Turn right down the minor road through the hamlet and after a left-hand bend, turn left to follow a Right of Way south up Chase End Hill. When close to the summit, turn left up the hill to the summit Trig Point. Return by the outbound route to the minor road through Whiteleaved Oak. At the bend in the road, go left then right to follow the Right of Way which runs, in the woods, along the west side of Ragged Stone Hill back to the start.

Howler's Heath

Howler's Heath is a southern outlier of the main ridge of the Malverns.

About Howler's Heath

Howler's Heath is the only one of the Malvern Hills which is in the county of Gloucestershire.

Height	90m/300ft
Summit GR:	SO 751355
Map:	O/S Explorer 190
Hill Category:	Tump

Howler's Heath

On older maps Howler's Heath was called Howling Heath.

Legend records that this was one of the final places in England where wolves survived. The hill was named after their howling.

Walk Description

Howler's Heath could be combined with Ragged Stone Hill and Chase End Hill, but the area between Howler's Heath and its near neighbours is private land, so it is best to climb it separately. Start from the minor road to the south of Howler's Heath, grid reference SO749348. Follow a track which climbs through woods, then open access land. At the top of the hill, turn right through a gate to follow a track passing between fields and woodland. The high point is a few metres into the woodland to the right of the track.

Continue east on this track as it enters woodland, then turn right to follow the track south to the minor road. Turn right and walk approximately 600m along the minor road to return to the start.

Distance:	3km/2 miles
Height to Climb:	90m/300ft
Start:	SO 749348
Difficulty:	2

Climbing Howler's Heath

Malvern Hills

Worcestershire Beacon from Sugar Loaf

Suckley Hills

The Suckley Hills give an interesting walk over two wooded hills that are close neighbours.

About Suckley Hills

Suckley Hills is the highest point of the small group of hills that take its name. They are part of the Malvern Hills, although lower and wooded. They lie close to the Worcestershire Way near the village of Longley Green.

Height	170m/558ft
Summit GR:	SO 734522
Map:	O/S Explorer 204
Hill Category:	Tump

Walk Summary

This is a moderate walk of nearly 6km over two neighbouring hills in the woods near Suckley. Part of the walk follows the Worcestershire Way, the long-distance trail from Bewdley to Great Malvern.

Distance:	5.5km/3.5 miles
Height to Climb:	160m/500ft
Start:	SO 736505
Difficulty:	3

About Suckley Hills West Top

The West Top is directly across the valley from the main summit, a drop of nearly 150ft then a re-ascent of approximately 120ft.

Height	164m/537ft
Summit GR:	SO 730520
Map:	O/S Explorer 204
Hill Category:	Tump

Knapp & Patermill NR

The Knapp and Papermill Nature Reserve near Alfrick Pound is a Site of Special Scientific Interest, with woodlands, old valley meadows and orchards to explore. There is also a Visitor Centre.

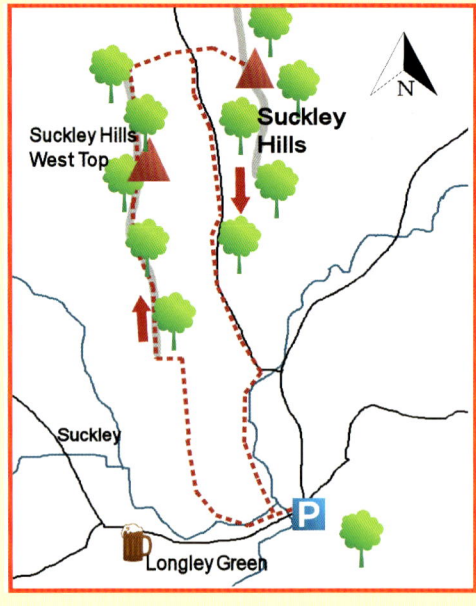

Malvern Hills

Walk Description

Suckley Hills from Upper Tundridge Farm

There is parking just east of Longley Green. From here walk west along the road into the village. Next to the Post Office a footpath (the Worcestershire Way) branches off to the right and goes north over the river. Follow the Worcestershire Way as it bends left towards the woodlands. Once in the woodlands the Worcestershire Way goes north. Continue following this going right at a junction.

The path continues, bending left after a few hundred metres to reach the top of the ridge through the woodlands. The path goes over a small hill, descends for about 50 metres, then makes its final climb to the summit of Suckley Hills West Top.

From the high point continue north on the path for 200m, then turn right, still following the Worcestershire Way signs, to descend through the trees. The path goes past an orchard, then crosses a lane and climbs east through the woodland. When the path reaches the ridge, turn left to follow the track for a short distance to the high point, which is on the ground to the right of the path.

Once at the high point, turn round and return to the lane between the two hills. Turn left along the lane and follow it for over one kilometre as it runs through the middle of the Suckley Hills.

At Upper Tunbridge Farm, a path goes off to the right. This path continues south, returning to the Post Office in Longley Green.

Gloucester & the Forest of Dean

Approaching the summit of May Hill

This area includes the Forest of Dean and the surrounding area, together with three interesting hills surrounding Gloucester.
The Forest of Dean is an area of over 100 square kilometres of ancient woodland between the Wye valley to the west and the Severn Valley to the East.

There are nineteen hills in total including well-known hills such as May Hill, the Buck Stone and Robins Wood Hill close to Gloucester.

May Hill Village Circular

The beautiful summit of May Hill is combined with Huntley Hill to give an interesting walk from May Hill Village.

About May Hill

May Hill is the highest hill in this section of the book with a beautiful clump of trees next to the summit Trig Point.

Height	296m/972ft
Summit GR:	SO 695213
Map:	O/S Explorer OL14
Hill Category:	Marilyn

Walk Summary

To combine May Hill and Huntley Hill, it is best to park in May Hill village, which lies between the two hills. It is normally possible to park at the Village Hall. From here, it is suggested that May Hill is climbed first.

Distance:	7 km/4.5 miles
Height to Climb:	240m/800ft
Start:	SO 708206
Difficulty:	3

About Huntley Hill

Huntley Hill is just south of May Hill village. Its summit is at the edge of woodland on a Right of Way.

Height	202m/663ft
Summit GR:	SO 703192
Map:	O/S Explorer OL14
Hill Category:	Tump

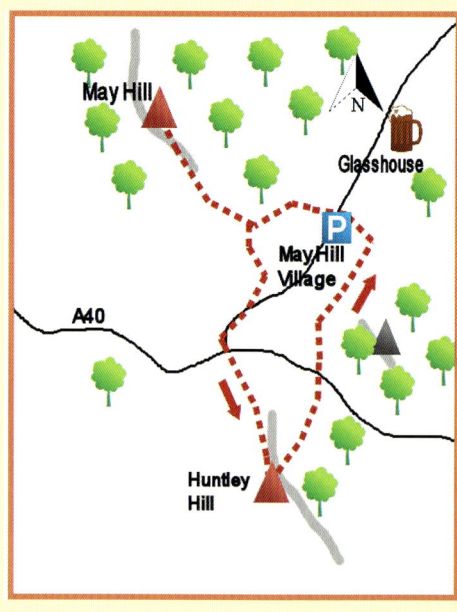

History of May Hill

May Hill can be picked out from long distances by the clump of trees on its summit. There are records of these trees dating back to the 18th Century. The dwindling clump was replenished in time for the Golden Jubilee of Queen Victoria. In 1935 the land passed into the care of the National Trust, and a further replenishment of the trees took place in 1977 for the silver jubilee of Elizabeth the Second.

Gloucester & the Forest of Dean

Walk Description

Summit of May Hill

Turn left out of the car park at the Village Hall and walk a short way down the road to join the Gloucestershire Way. When the Gloucestershire Way is reached, turn right to follow it uphill through the village. Follow the signs to continue on the Gloucestershire Way and, in under two kilometres, the summit of May Hill with its clump of trees appears.

Return by the same route for 800m. On reaching a minor road, turn right to follow the road south, then go right at a fork to continue south towards Dursley Cross Farm. At another minor road, turn left, then turn right after a short distance. This minor road joins the A40. Cross the A40 and a short distance to the right, there is a public footpath sign. Take this footpath which climbs south through fields to Huntley Hill Wood. On arriving at Huntley Hill Wood, turn right and walk for a few metres to the highest point.

Return north on this track following it beside the edge of the wood. It heads directly towards May Hill village. When it reaches the A40, turn right then immediately left to follow a minor road north towards May Hill village. When the minor road forks, take the right-hand one to return to the car.

Wigpool Common

To the west of the small town of Mitcheldean, lies high ground topped by the attractive summit of Wigpool Common.

About Wigpool Common

Wigpool Common lies above Mitcheldean. Its summit Trig Point is in woods.

Height	279m/915ft
Summit GR:	SO 655192
Map:	O/S Explorer OL14
Hill Category:	Tump

Walk Description

The start point is the car park at the centre of Mitcheldean, which lies just east of the B4224, on the opposite side of the road from the church (Grid Ref SO 664186). Cross the road and walk past the right side of the church. Turn right just past the church and follow the lane to a Right of Way. When the path forks, take the left-hand fork, which goes through a gate, then climbs the hill heading for the left-hand side of a small wood. Follow the path past the left-hand side of the wood, continuing until a road is reached. Turn right along the road. After 200 metres there is a house on the right. The Trig Point is 20 metres into the wood on the left side.

Summit of Wigpool Common

Chase Wood Hill

A climb to the summit of Ross-on-Wye's local hill

About Chase Wood Hill

Chase Wood Hill rises steeply just to the south of Ross-on-Wye and is popular with local people. It is an unusual hill with a summit meadow, and steep wooded slopes.

Height	203m/666ft
Summit GR:	SO 602225
Map:	O/S Explorer OL14
Hill Category:	Hump

Meadows on Chase Wood

Hill Fort on Chase Hill

Chase Hill has some of the earliest evidence of human activity in the Ross area, in the form of flint tools. By the Iron Age the hill had become an important hill fort. The main period of occupation seems to have been from the 5th or 4th century BC when earthwork defences covered 19 acres and housed maybe 1,400 people. The site was probably abandoned after the Roman invasion.

Walk Description

The shortest ascent starts from the top of the lane near Hill Farm (grid reference SO604229). From here tracks lead south-west through the wood until close to the Trig Point. The Trig Point is in the meadow ten metres from the edge of the wood. The edge of the wood is the same height as the summit so there is no need to go into the meadow.

There are numerous other options for ascending Chase Wood Hill. The Wye Valley walk goes from the Centre of Ross-on-Wye to the edge of the summit meadow (2.5km). Equally the Wye Valley walk could be used to ascend from the south (1.5km).

A popular route is to park at Fernbank road (grid reference SO598231). Follow the road and lane to Hill Farm, then follow the tracks leading south-west (as for the shortest ascent described in paragraph one of the walk description).

Littledean Hills

A woodland and heathland walk on the east edge of the Forest of Dean.

About Edge Hills

Edge Hills is the highest of these hills and lies in woodland near radio masts.

Height	281m/920ft
Summit GR:	SO 663160
Map:	O/S Explorer OL14
Hill Category:	Tump

About Chestnuts Hill

Chestnuts Hill has a Trig Point and Well at its summit. The hill is in woods just east of Pope's Hill village.

Height	196m/643ft
Summit GR:	SO 679146
Map:	O/S Explorer OL14
Hill Category:	Tump

About Hangman's Hill

Hangman's Hill lies just north of Chestnuts Hill next to a Right of Way

Height	180m/591ft
Summit GR:	SO 678154
Map:	O/S Explorer OL14
Hill Category:	Tump

Walk Summary

The walk starts at Pope's Hill village just east of Chestnuts Hill. From here, it is a short climb through the woods to the Trig Point at the top of Chestnuts Hill. The walk continues west through woods, then over heathland to the masts at the top of Edge Hills. On the return journey the walk deviates north to take in Hangman's Hill, which is in woods to the north of Chestnuts Hill.

Distance:	9 km/5.5 miles
Height to Climb:	330m/1,100ft
Start:	SO 685146
Difficulty:	4

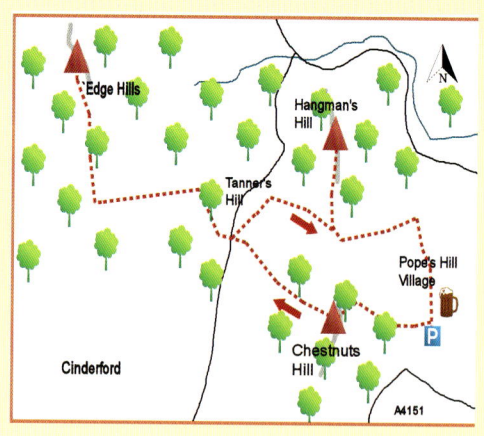

Gloucester & the Forest of Dean

Walk Description

Edge Hills from Chestnuts Hills

The walk starts at Pope's Hill village. Walk west directly towards Chestnuts Hill. When the road bends left, take the right-hand track which climbs through the woods. After 250m, a track goes left up the hill. Follow this to the summit where there is a Trig Point and Well.

From the summit, follow tracks north-west down the wooded hillside. After 400m a house appears on the left. Before a gate and the house drive, turn right on a footpath. After 400m, the track reaches a road junction. Cross over the road junction and follow a track which goes north-west on the other side of the road. After 300m, opposite some buildings, turn left to follow a Right of Way west up the hillside. This reaches a minor road after a further 400m. From the road a path runs north to the radio masts at the summit of Edge Hills.

From the summit, return to the road junction between Edge Hills and Chestnuts Hill. At the road junction, take the minor road which runs north-east past a farm on the right-hand side. Just past the entrance to the farm, a path goes east through fields to pass between Chestnuts Hill and Hangman's Hill.

At the top of the pass between the two hills, turn left to follow a path to the summit of Hangman's Hill. The summit is unmarked, but is the high point of Welshbury Hill Fort, an old Iron Age hill fort. This is reputed to be the place where the Celtic Dobunni tribe staged its last battle against the Romans after a long running guerrilla war.

From the high point return to the pass between the two hills, then turn left to descend. Keep to the right on the descent to return to Pope's Hill village.

Staple Edge Hill

A walk through the Forest of Dean south of Cinderford.

About Staple Edge Hill

This hill lies near Staple Edge Bungalows and can be approached from Cinderford, Upper Soudley, or Mallards Pike Lake to the south.

Height	228m/748ft
Summit GR:	SO 646104
Map:	O/S Explorer OL14
Hill Category:	Tump

Walk Summary

There is parking near Mallards Pike Lake which lies south-west of Staple Edge Hill (charge). The suggested route goes north-east from the car park to the summit of Staple Edge Hill.

Distance:	5 km/3 miles
Height to Climb:	120m/400ft
Start:	SO 636093
Difficulty:	2

Mallards Pike Lake

Mallards Pike Lake and the surrounding area is owned by Forestry England. The facilities include Mallards Pike café, toilets, and a picnic area. The activities include 'Go Ape tree top challenge' and cycling and running trails. The Yellow trail goes close to the summit of Staple Edge Hill

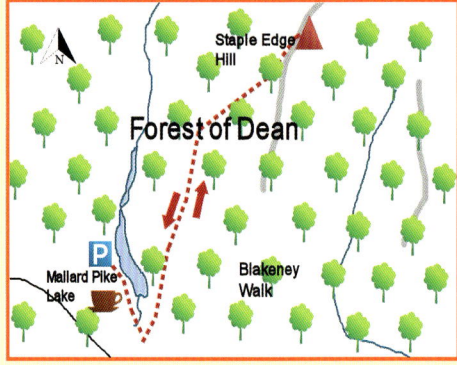

Buildings near the summit of Staple Edge Hill

Gloucester & the Forest of Dean

Walk Description

Mallards Pike Lake

From the car park, walk round the south end of Mallards Pike Lake, then follow a track which runs north a couple of hundred feet above the lake. At Nine Wells, fork right to climb north-east up the hillside. After approximately 800 metres, Staple Edge Bungalows appears on the right. The high point is undefined just north of the buildings.

Return by the same route to the south end of Mallards Pike Lake and back to the car park.

Staple Edge Hill can be climbed via a shorter route from the west end of Upper Soudley, but the opportunity to explore the surrounds of Mallards Lake would be lost.

Blaze Bailey

A hill walk offering a splendid viewpoint over the River Severn.

About Blaze Bailey

Blaze Bailey is one of the closest hills to the River Severn and an excellent viewpoint.

Height	208m/682ft
Summit GR:	SO 669116
Map:	O/S Explorer OL14
Hill Category:	Tump

Walk Description

Park at the Soudley Ponds car park on the minor road from Littledean to Upper Soudley. From the north end of the car park follow tracks east directly up the hillside to the forest track which runs along the summit ridge. The high point is 30 metres east of the forest track on a small ridge.

To visit the viewpoint, walk north on the forest track for approximately 500m and take a right turn. After 50 metres the viewpoint over the River Severn appears. Now return to the forest track and continue north for a short distance. The track bends left on its descent. After 100m, carry straight on when a track goes off to the left. After a further 100m a second track goes off to the left. Follow this track which leads back to the car park.

Distance:	3 km/2 miles
Height to Climb:	120m/400ft
Start:	SO 663116
Difficulty:	2

Soudley Ponds

The ponds, which lie next to the car park at the start of the walk, are believed to have been dug in the 18th century to provide water to the furnaces in the Soudley Valley. They are now popular with bird watchers and are surrounded by Douglas Fir trees.

It is also worth visiting the nearby Dean Heritage Centre with its museum, café and various outside displays.

Gloucester & the Forest of Dean

Soudley Ponds

Crabtree Hill in the 'Dean'

A walk from Cinderford through the northern part of the Forest of Dean.

About Crabtree Hill

This hill lies just west of Cinderford with the high point close to a junction of paths.

Height	203m/666ft
Summit GR:	SO 633137
Map:	O/S Explorer OL14
Hill Category:	Tump

Walk Summary

This is a walk through the Forest of Dean from Cinderford on forest tracks and along the Wysis Way. The Wysis Way is a long-distance footpath from Monmouth to the beginning of the Thames Path.

Distance:	8.5 km/5 miles
Height to Climb:	120m/400ft
Start:	SO 650139
Difficulty:	3

About Serridge Inclosure

This hill lies in the northern part of the Forest of Dean on a hillock within the woodland.

Height	207m/679ft
Summit GR:	SO 621143
Map:	O/S Explorer OL14
Hill Category:	Tump

Forest of Dean

The Forest of Dean is characterised by over 100 square kilometres of mixed woodland, one of the ancient woodlands in England. A large area was reserved as a royal hunting ground before 1066, and it remains the second largest crown forest in England, after the New Forest. The main sources of work are forestry, iron working and coal mining. The main towns are Cinderford in the east, Coleford in the west, and Lydney in the south of the area.

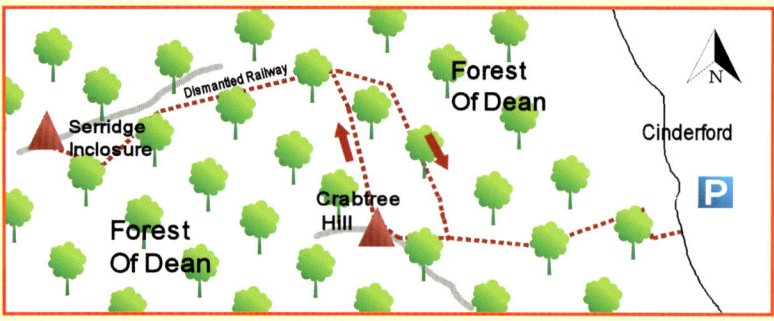

Gloucester & the Forest of Dean

Walk Description

Near the summit of Crabtree Hill

The walk starts from Cinderford. Park near the roundabout on Valley Road on the west side of Cinderford. Just south of the roundabout, a rough road runs west towards a café. Follow this, turn right after 300m and follow the road north. After 200m a good forest track goes west. Follow this for 1.5km to a junction of tracks on the edge of the woodland - shown by the photo above.

This is generally considered to be the summit of Crabtree Hill, although the ground a couple of hundred metres west is slightly higher. From here follow a track north for 1km to join the Wysis Way at a dismantled railway. Turn left and follow the Wysis Way for 1km until higher ground can be seen directly ahead. Leave the Wysis Way and climb to the summit of Serridge Inclosure on the higher ground.

The return journey can be made by the same route. A variation can be made by following route 42 past Crump Meadow enclosure. This is a slightly shorter route back to the car.

Little Doward & Coppet Hill

These two hills lie in the Wye Valley Area of Outstanding Natural Beauty, and give a good day out, which could be combined with a visit to Goodrich Castle. The hills are west of the River Wye and comprise two of the five hills in this book in Herefordshire.

About Little Doward

Little Doward lies in woodland south of Symonds Yat. It is a straightforward climb from parking north-west of the summit.

Height	222m/730ft
Summit GR:	SO 539161
Map:	O/S Explorer OL14
Hill Category:	Hump

About Coppet Hill

Coppet Hill lies on heathland above the village of Goodrich. Its ascent could be combined with a visit to Goodrich Castle.

Height	201m/659ft
Summit GR:	SO 577181
Map:	O/S Explorer OL14
Hill Category:	Hump

Walk Summary

Little Doward is climbed from the car park at Long Close Wood, just off the A40. From the car park, follow the forestry tracks which break out of the woods near the summit. A small path goes off to the left to the Trig Point.

Coppet Hill can be climbed from Goodrich or Goodrich Castle car park. A good track leaves Goodrich and climbs the hill to the Trig Point and high point at the Folly.

These are two separate walks on either side of Symonds Yat, combined due to their close proximity.

Goodrich Castle

Standing high on a rocky cliff, Goodrich Castle appears to have been carved from one enormous chunk of red sandstone. It was built around 1086, with additions to the building being made in the late 13th Century. It featured prominently in the English Civil War, eventually being taken by the Parliamentarians. It is currently owned by English Heritage and can be visited before or after climbing Coppet Hill.

Gloucester & the Forest of Dean

Walk Descriptions

View from Coppet Hill

Little Doward

To climb Little Doward, leave the A40 at the exit about two miles north of Monmouth signposted for Little Doward and Great Doward. Follow the signs to Little Doward and, after a few hundred metres, a car park appears on the right. Park here and follow a forest track which zig-zags up the hillside, climbing steadily. Near the summit, the track breaks out of the woodland (see photo opposite).

From the high point of the track, a path goes off to the left. After 100m it reaches the Trig Point, which can be seen from the track.

Coppet Hill

Coppet Hill can be climbed from the centre of Goodrich village or from the car park at Goodrich Castle (which adds one kilometre to the distance). From Goodrich Castle car park, walk into the village, then walk south on a minor road, directly towards the hillside.

After a few hundred metres, the road splits into two. From just behind this junction, a path goes up the hillside, steeply at first. Follow the path as it passes a house, then breaks into beautiful open hillside. The Trig Point is reached first. Continue climbing for another 100m to a folly, which looks like a broken wall, to complete the hill.

Ruardean Hill

The highest point in the Forest of Dean lies on the outskirts of village from where the name is taken.

Ruardean Hill

Ruardean Hill is the second highest hill in this geographical section, after May Hill.

Height	290m/951ft
Summit GR:	SO 635169
Map:	O/S Explorer OL14
Hill Category:	Marilyn

Walk Description

Ruardean Hill lies near Ruardean Hill Sports Club (follow sat-nav to GL17 9AR). Very little walking is required as the summit is next to a Flagpole about fifty metres from the Sports Club.

After bagging the summit next to the flagpole, it is worth making the short walk to the viewpoint and the memorial to the miners in the Country Park approximately 200m to the north.

Pan Tod Beacon

Summit Features

Near the summit of Ruardean Hill is a beacon and two miners memorials.

Pan Tod Beacon was built in 2002 and is lit to commemorate important occasions such as the recent coronation of King Charles 111.

The statue of the crouching miner and the memorial to miners killed in mining accidents were added in 2008 and 2017 respectively.

Gloucester & the Forest of Dean

Near Summit of Blakes Wood (see pps 70 & 71)

Staunton Hills

Buck Stone and Blake's Wood can be visited in two short walks from the village of Staunton.

About Buck Stone

Buck Stone is an iconic summit in the far west of Gloucestershire near the Welsh border. It is a straightforward walk to the top.

Height	280m/917ft
Summit GR:	SO 542123
Map:	O/S Explorer OL14
Hill Category:	Hump

Walk Summary

This is the combination of two short walks on good paths from the village of Staunton, which lies on the A4136 a few miles east of Monmouth

Distance:	4.5 km/2.5 miles
Height to Climb:	120m/400ft
Start:	SO 548127
Difficulty:	2

Author at Buck Stone c: John Roberts

About Blake's Wood

On the opposite side of the valley from the Buck Stone lies Blake's Wood.

Height	243m/797ft
Summit GR:	SO 554121
Map:	O/S Explorer OL14
Hill Category:	Tump

The Buck Stone

The Buck Stone, after which the hill is named, lies just to the west of the summit Trig Point. It is a naturally occurring stone which originally rocked but was cemented into place after an accident in the nineteenth century. The stone appears to have been hollowed out in the middle and may have been used for sacrifice. It looks west over the Welsh hills.

Gloucester & the Forest of Dean

Walk Descriptions

Summit of Buck Stone

Park in Staunton village near the White Horse Inn, or in the White Horse car park if eating or drinking there.

To climb Buck Stone, walk 100m west along the A4136 from the White Horse Inn to find a lane branching off to the left. Follow the lane 100m to a left-hand bend, and immediately after the bend, a footpath branches off to the right. This footpath is followed through woods to the Trig Point and large stone (see picture) at the summit. The Buck Stone (see the photo on the opposite page) is on the edge of the escarpment. Return to the White Horse by continuing past the Trig Point. The path drops down to a lane. Turn left and follow the lane back to the start.

From the White Horse, walk east through the village to the church. Opposite the church, a public footpath runs south-east to Blake's Wood. Follow this as it climbs into the wood. The summit is soon reached, the high point is in the woods just east of the footpath.

Sandhurst Hill

This small hill combines a viewpoint with a walk along the Severn Way.

About Sandhurst Hill

At under 100m Sandhurst Hill is the lowest hill in this listing and lies close to the River Severn.

Height	88m/288ft
Summit GR:	SO 839250
Map:	O/S Explorer 179
Hill Category:	Tump

The Severn Way

The Severn Way runs 337km (210 miles) along the Severn Valley from the source of the river to the sea. It starts on the wild Plynlimon plateau in mid Wales (see the Welsh mountains app 'Y Marilyns' which includes Plynlimon). The route passes through Welshpool and Shrewsbury before heading south through Worcester, Tewkesbury and Gloucester to Severn Beach.

Walk Description

Start from near the Red Lion pub on Wainlode Lane near Bishop's Norton (postcode GL2 9LW). Follow the Severn Way for a short distance west. When the woods are reached, turn left on a path up the hillside.

The path continues south-west up the hill until, after about 200ft of climbing, the wide summit ridge is reached. Follow the summit ridge to the Trig Point and table and chairs. About 300m before the Trig Point, the high point is passed although this is only marginally higher than the Trig Point.

There are three possible routes of descent, return by the same route, turn left to descend to Bishop's Norton and left again on reaching Bishop's Norton, or return by the Severn Way. The return by the Severn Way, although longer, is my preferred route. Continue following the path west from the Trig Point. After just over 1km, turn right at Brawn Farm, and follow Rodway Lane to the Severn Way next to the River Severn. Finally follow the Severn Way east for 3.5km to return to the start.

Distance:	9 km/5.5 miles
Height to Climb:	80m/270ft
Start:	SO 848258
Difficulty:	3

Churchdown Hill

Woodland, a medieval church and summit views make this a place for all the family to explore.

About Churchdown Hill

Churchdown Hill lies close to Gloucester and is sometimes known as Chosen Hill or Tinker's Hill.

Height	155m/509ft
Summit GR:	SO 880188
Map:	O/S Explorer 179
Hill Category:	Hump

History of Churchdown Hill

Churchdown Hill is the site of an Iron Age hill fort, and an early medieval church, St Bartholomew's. In 1471 Edward the fourth sent his scouts to the top of the hill before the Battle of Tewkesbury, where he defeated Margaret of Anjou and kept the crown for many years thereafter.

Walk Description

Churchdown Hill can be climbed by driving up to St Bartholomew's Church, walking west past the graveyards, continuing through a gate, then turning left to the viewfinder. The distance is only 300 metres to the viewfinder.

A longer walk starts from near the church in Churchdown. From here follow the minor road south-west for 250m to a right-angle bend, then join a footpath which climbs the hill. After the footpath enters the woods, turn left to follow a path to the summit. The route of descent can be varied so that St Bartholomew's Church is passed on the way down.

Distance:	2.5 km/1.5 miles
Height to Climb:	100m/330ft
Start:	SO 884196
Difficulty:	2

Summit of Churchdown Hill

Robins Wood Hill

Robins Wood Hill dominates the south-east side of Gloucester rising 500ft above the valley floor and giving the opportunity for multiple walks through the Country Park and Nature Reserve.

About Robins Wood Hill

A justifiably popular hill close to the centre of Gloucester.

Height	198m/650ft
Summit GR:	SO 841150
Map:	O/S Explorer 179
Hill Category:	Hump

History of Robins Hood Hill

There has been human occupation on Robins Wood Hill for at least 4,000 years. It supplied drinking water to Gloucester from the 12th Century until 1946. Robins Wood Hill has been a Country Park since 1972. It is also now a local nature reserve. There are several footpaths and nature trails on the hill. On the east side of the hill there is a dry ski slope and golf course.

Walk Description

There is a substantial car park, a café and a play area just north of the hill. The car park is just off the A38 on the south side of Gloucester. Follow signs to Robinswood and Robinswood Hill Country Park.

From the car park there are a variety of routes to the top of the hill. Follow any of the paths heading south and south-east up the hill and continue climbing for approximately 1km. The summit, with its viewfinder, Trig Point and beacon, can be seen when the path breaks out of the wood. From the summit, follow the ridge south for 200m to see the views south to Stroud and the Severn Estuary. Return to the car park by the same or a similar route.

Distance:	2.5 km/1.5 miles
Height to Climb:	150m/500ft
Start:	SO 836157
Difficulty:	2

Gloucester & the Forest of Dean

The Cotswolds

The Cotswolds cover an area of 800 square kilometres, mainly in Gloucestershire and Oxfordshire. The hills run from the market town of Broadway in the north to the market town of Dursley in the south. There are sixteen hills featured below including the highest hill in the Cotswolds, Cleeve Hill near Cheltenham. The section also includes the second highest hill, Seven Wells Hill, near Broadway, historic Leckhampton Hill, and a group of three hills near Dursley including Cam Long Down. Twelve of the sixteen hills are very close or on the Cotswolds Way, a long-distance route from Chipping Campden to Bath.

Broadway Tower

Seven Wells & Shenbarrow

A classic circuit from Broadway including a visit to the iconic Broadway Tower.

About Seven Wells Hill

Seven Wells Hill is the second highest hill in Gloucestershire. The top of the Broadway Tower is marginally higher than the true summit. However, the land on which it stands is six metres lower than the top of Seven Wells Hill a mile to the south.

Height	319m/1,047ft
Summit GR:	SP 115348
Map:	O/S Explorer OL45
Hill Category:	Hump

Walk Summary

This is an interesting circular walk from the centre of Broadway. It is all on good tracks or lanes and passes Broadway Tower, the attractive village of Snowshill and the lavender fields. There is an option of a stop for coffee or lunch at the Broadway Country Park.

Distance:	13 km/8 miles
Height to Climb:	300m/1,000ft
Start:	SP 100377
Difficulty:	4

About Shenbarrow Hill

Shenberrow Hill lies across the valley from Seven Wells Hill. It is the third highest point in Gloucestershire.

Height	304m/997ft
Summit GR:	SP 084333
Map:	O/S Explorer OL45
Hill Category:	Tump

Broadway Tower & Country Park

The Broadway Tower was created in the 18th Century by the landscape designer 'Capability Brown'. It was completed in 1798 by James Wyatt with a dramatic outlook and wide-ranging views. The roof viewing platform has views spanning 16 counties. The Broadway Tower is attached to a two-hundred-acre Country Park with deer, a restaurant and shop.

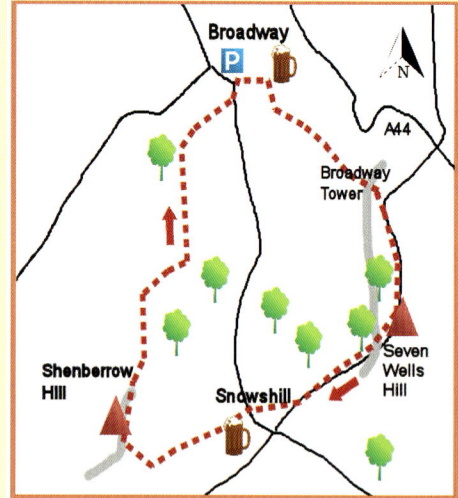

The Cotswolds

Walk Description

Broadway

The walk starts from the centre of Broadway where there is parking (charge). From the centre of Broadway near the Swan Inn, walk east up the High Street carrying on to Upper High Street. After walking up Upper High Street for 200 metres, turn right to follow the Cotswold Way (sign). This heads south then south-east up a hill towards Broadway Tower.

After nearly 2km, Broadway Tower is reached. Not far from Broadway Tower is the Country Park and restaurant, where refreshments are available. To continue to the summit of Seven Wells Hill, walk south down the minor road passing the Country Park which is on the right. After just over 1km and 200 metres before a T junction, the high point of Seven Wells Hill is passed. It is next to a wall about 50 metres to the east of the road, but on private land.

Continue to the T junction, then turn right following signs to Snowshill and Snowshill lavender fields. The minor road descends to Snowshill. On entering Snowshill go straight over at a crossroads and pass a church on your right.

Seven Wells & Shenbarrow

Walk Description (cont)

Snowshill is a beautiful Cotswolds country village, with a 16th Century Country House, Snowshill Manor, now owned by the National Trust. Charles Wade gave the Manor to the National Trust in 1951, together with an eclectic collection of thousands of objects.

After passing the church bear left up the hill. After a few hundred metres go right at a junction of the road. Continue up the hill for a further 400 metres. When the road goes off to the right, there is a sign indicating the continuation of the Winchcombe Way by a path through the field. Follow this path to the wide summit ridge of Shenberrow Hill. Turn right on a track going south.

After 100 metres the summit of Shenberrow Hill is passed, near an old disused building. Continue south on the track for another 2km to join the Cotswolds Way. This leads back to Broadway. Turn left when entering Broadway (opposite a church) and follow Snowshill Road for a short distance back to the start.

The Cotswold Way

The Cotswold Way runs from Chipping Campden in the north to Bath in the south. It follows the Cotswolds escarpment for much of the route and has a length of 164km (102 miles). It passes ancient sites, beautiful villages, and has some good views as it passes through woodland and meadows.

Descending to Snowshill

Nut Hill

Take an evening stroll from Upton St Leonards or Bowden Hall Hotel to the summit of Nut Hill with its Second World War pill box and underground bunker.

Walk Description

It is a short walk from the Bowden Hall Hotel to the summit of Nut Hill. If using the facilities of the Bowden Hall Hotel, park in the hotel car park, otherwise park nearby in Upper St Leonards, and walk to Bowden Hall car park.

A path leaves the east side of the car park (the left side as seen from the car park entrance). This path climbs the hill to the strange summit with the pill box and bunker.

Distance: 1 km/0.6 miles
Height to Climb: 45m/150ft
Start: SO 872151
Difficulty: 1

About Nut Hill

Nut Hill is on access land between Cheltenham and Gloucester.

Height 119m/390ft
Summit GR: SO 874150
Map: O/S Explorer 179
Hill Category: Tump

History of Nut Hill

In the late 19th Century, an ornamental stone summer house was erected on the summit. By the 1930s the summer house had disappeared. During the Second World War, two structures were erected, a five sided 'pill box' gun emplacement and an underground bunker with an access shaft, flu and ventilation shaft.

Summit of Nut Hill

Swell Hill

This is a circular walk from Stow-on-the-Wold past Lower Swell and Upper Swell to a Trig Point on an old Roman road.

About Swell Hill

Swell Hill is the highest point of the Cotswolds between Stow and Temple Guisling.

Height	235m/771ft
Summit GR:	SP 155267
Map:	O/S Explorer OL45
Hill Category:	Tump

Walk Summary

This is a 10km circular walk going west from Stow-on-the-Wold, passing Lower Swell on the way to Swell Hill, following the old Roman road north, then returning on the Gloucestershire Way.

Distance:	10 km/6 miles
Height to Climb:	180m/600ft
Start:	SP 190257
Difficulty:	3

Stow-on-the-Wold

Stow stands at the top of an 800ft hill at the junction of two main roads which pass through the Cotswolds.

The hill is not featured in this book as it is in the middle of the town and difficult to access.

Stow-on-the-Wold has an extensive history including a battle between Royalists and Parliamentary forces in 1646 and large scale trading in sheep in the 18th century.

More recently it has been featured in 'Top Gear'.

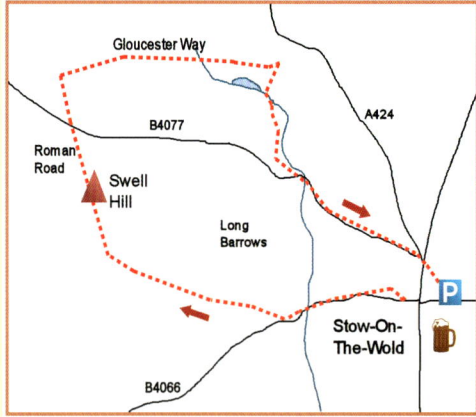

The Cotswolds

Walk Description

Summit of Swell Hill

Park in Stow-on-the-Wold and walk to the crossroads in the middle of the town. The highest point in the town and the summit of Stow-on-the-Wold hill is 200 metres south of the crossroads near the cemetery.

From the crossroads follow a path next to the B4068 down the hill to Lower Swell. In Lower Swell take the right fork at the junction and continue west on a minor road up the hill. Ignore signs to Upper Swell. After 1.5km at the top of the hill, a good track goes off to the right. This is the old Roman road. For a few hundred metres the track rises slowly to the Trig Point of Swell Hill.

Continue north past the Trig Point and start descending. Cross the B4077 and continue along the Roman road for another 400m. Turn right on a minor road which soon joins the Gloucestershire Way. The Gloucestershire Way is now followed back to Stow-on-the-Wold. After walking 2km on the minor road, a right turn leads to the village of Upper Swell. From Upper Swell, the Gloucestershire Way climbs back to Stow-on-the-Wold

Swell Hill is a short walk from the B4077 road between Stow and Temple Guiting and could be climbed in this way. However, the walk suggested is an interesting hike through the Cotswolds with refreshments in Stow-on-the-Wold at the start and end of the walk.

Cleeve Hill

It is a short walk from the Radio Masts car park to Cleeve Hill summit, but the walk should be extended to explore Cleeve Common.

About Cleeve Hill

Cleeve Hill is the highest point in the Cotswolds.

Height	330m/1,083ft
Summit GR:	SO 997246
Map:	O/S Explorer 179
Hill Category:	Marilyn

Walk Summary

The shortest route to the summit of Cleeve Hill, the highest point in Gloucestershire, starts at the Radio Masts car park (grid reference SO 994249). However, the featured walk starts from the Quarry Car Park.

Distance:	8 km/5 miles
Height to Climb:	150m/500ft
Start:	SP 989272
Difficulty:	2

Actual summit of Cleeve Hill and the 3 Masts

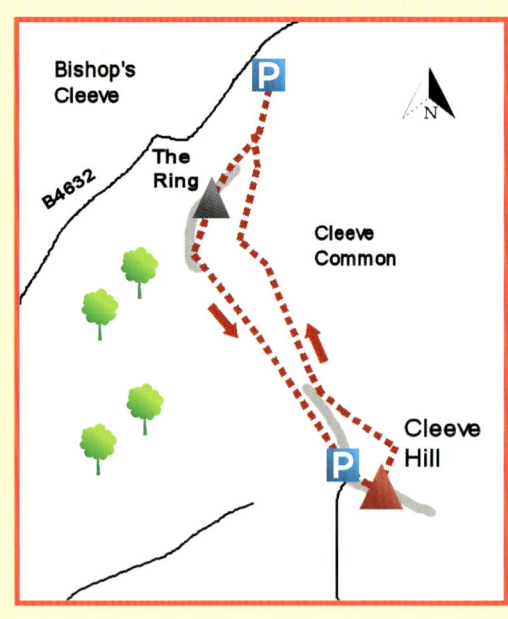

The Cotswolds

Walk Description

False summits of Cleeve Hill

Probably the best walk to the summit of Cleeve Hill and one that explores Cleeve Common starts at the Quarry car park near Cleeve Hill golf club (nearest postcode reference GL52 3PW). This gives a walk of approximately 8km following the Cotswold Way on the outward journey and the Winchcombe Way on the return journey.

From the car park follow the Cotswold Way south to the Trig Point above The Ring. The Ring is a circular earthwork that may have served as an enclosure for animals in the early centuries AD. This Trig Point is not the summit but is a good viewpoint.

Continue south-west on the Cotswold Way for approximately 250m, then turn left and head south-east on a path which goes directly towards the three masts in the distance. After 1.5km arrive at the masts. Continue past these masts and past the car park (which is just to the right) to reach the summit Trig Point.

To vary the return journey, return to the car park, then walk north-east for 250m to join the Winchcombe Way. This runs north-north-west, then north back to the car park.

Leckhampton Hill

A hill with a long history and outstanding views over Cheltenham.

About Leckhampton Hill

At just under 1,000ft Leckhampton Hill dominates the south side of Cheltenham.

Height	293m/961ft
Summit GR:	SO 949184
Map:	O/S Explorer 179
Hill Category:	Tump

Walk Summary

There are many routes up Cheltenham's local hill. There are car parks to the north, south, and south-east of the summit. The easiest ascent is from the car park to the south-east of the summit.

Distance:	2 km/1.3 miles
Height to Climb:	15m/50ft
Start:	SP 951179
Difficulty:	1

History of Leckhampton Hill

Leckhampton Hill was a burial place and settlement site in the Iron Age. In medieval times, it was a sheep run, then it was quarried for natural resources in the 18th and 19th centuries. Following disputes over access in the early 20th century, Cheltenham Borough Council purchased the hill in 1927 and opened it to the public in 1929. It is now a popular place for recreational activities near the centre of Cheltenham.

Distinctive Trig Point of Leckhampton Hill

The Cotswolds

Walk Description

View over Cheltenham

From the south-east car park the direct route towards the summit is blocked by the quarry, but a path goes uphill to the right of the quarry. After 100m, when this path joins the main path up the hill, turn left and follow the well-maintained gravel path. This path is followed all the way to the summit Trig Point (see below), a distance of approximately one kilometre.

In addition to the Trig Point, an Iron Age hill fort and a viewfinder can be found on the summit area. The route can be varied on the descent by continuing in an easterly direction, then bending round to the right to return to the car park.

Crickley & Birdlip Hill

A high-level walk over two hills close to the Cotswold Way, south of Cheltenham.

About Birdlip Hill

At a height of 300m, Birdlip Hill is the highest point in South Gloucestershire. The summit is defined by a Trig Point and covered reservoir.

Height	300m/983ft
Summit GR:	SO 925141
Map:	O/S Explorer 179
Hill Category:	Hump

Walk Summary

This walk follows the Cotswold Way for two-thirds of its distance. The walk starts at Barrow Wake car park between the two hills. It goes north to Crickley Hill Country Park, then heads south to Birdlip Hill. Refreshments are available at Crickley Hill Country Park and Birdlip.

Distance:	8 km/5 miles
Height to Climb:	150m/500ft
Start:	SO 931153
Difficulty:	3

About Crickley Hill

Crickley Hill sits in its own Country Park with good views west.

Height	273m/896ft
Summit GR	SO 931164
Map:	O/S Explorer 179
Hill Category:	Tump

Crickley Hill Country Park

The park lies on the Cotswold Escarpment and is jointly owned by the National Trust and Gloucestershire Wildlife Trust. It has a café, a visitors' centre and is the location of a hill fort first built around 5,000 years ago and rebuilt many times. It is also the scene of one of the first battles in England.

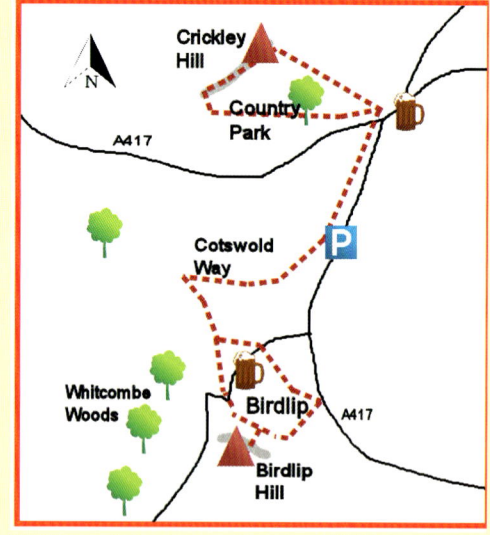

The Cotswolds

Walk Description

Approaching Crickley Hill on the Cotswold Way

The walk starts at Barrow Wake car park just off the A417, sat-nav reference GL4 8JY. Follow the Cotswold Way north for 800m as it runs close to the A417. The Cotswold Way crosses the busy A417 near a roundabout (take care), then enters the Crickley Hill Country Park. It follows the edge of the Cotswold escarpment west, then north-east, and arrives at the Crickley Hill car park and café. Continue north-east on the Cotswold Way for 300m to the top of Crickley Hill next to the coach park.

A footpath runs east through trees from just south of the coach park to exit the Country Park and rejoin the Cotswolds Way next to the A417 roundabout. Cross the A417 and walk south on the Cotswold Way past the car park. Continue south-west with good views over the edge of the escarpment.

Approximately 1km past the car park, the Cotswold Way turns south-east and heads directly towards Birdlip. After 300m, turn left along a footpath which crosses the B4070. After another 200m, the path splits. Take the path which goes south, directly to the village of Birdlip.

Turn right when the road is reached, then left past a church. Finally, on exiting the village, turn right to follow a path to the Trig Point and covered reservoir.

Return to the road, turn left to pass the church, then left again to walk through the middle of Birdlip past the Royal George. At a junction in the road, carry straight on down the hill. The road bears to the right and the Cotswold Way leaves the road to head north. The outward route is rejoined and the Cotswold Way is followed back to the car park.

Painswick Beacon

The summit of Painswick Beacon is next to the sixth tee of the golf course.

About Painswick Beacon

A high summit in Gloucestershire near the attractive town of Painswick.

Height	283m/928ft
Summit GR:	SO 868120
Map:	O/S Explorer 179
Hill Category:	Tump

Walk Description

Turn left off the B4073 road from Gloucester to Painswick when west of the summit and follow a minor road for a short distance to a parking area.

Walk south beside the road for a short distance until the road crosses the golf course. Turn left to follow the Wysis Way north. The path runs along the left-hand side of the golf course. Continue north to the Trig Point. It is quickest to return the same way, a walk of 1.5km (1 mile). However, the walk can be extended by continuing east round the left-hand side of the golf course and returning to the start along the Cotswold Way.

Approaching the summit of Painswick Beacon

Minchinhampton Common

Take a walk amongst golfers and cows on Minchinhampton Common.

About Minchinhampton Common

This large attractive common is complete with a fine golf course. The highest point is difficult to pinpoint.

Height	207m/679ft
Summit GR:	SO 854016
Map:	O/S Explorer 168
Hill Category:	Tump

Walk Description

There is National Trust parking near the Reservoir (SO 855013). From here it is a short and flat walk of about 400m, north then a short distance west, to the high point 50m south of one of the greens on the golf course. In total the walk is therefore 800m.

The walk can be expanded to see more of Minchinhampton Common, which is one of the largest grassland commons in the Cotswold area. The Common has been the site of Prehistoric fields and defensive sites, medieval roads, hollow ways and turnpike systems, and World War Two defences.

On Minchinhampton Common

Doverow Hill

The Cotswold Way passes close to this wooded summit near Stroud.

About Doverow Hill

Doverow Hill is a prominent summit in woodland near Stroud.

Height	143m/469ft
Summit GR:	SO 816053
Map:	O/S Explorer 179
Hill Category:	Tump

Walk Description

Doverow Hill lies near Stroud and can be climbed from a number of directions. A good circular walk starts from the B4008 directly south of the summit. Roadside parking can be found in this area. A sign marks the place where the Cotswold Way goes north from the B4008. Follow this and cross a footbridge over the railway. The path swings right and passes through an apple orchard.

After a few hundred metres a track leaves the Cotswold Way and heads west for the wooded summit of the hill. Follow the track to the woods, then take the high track through the left side of the woods. This passes the unmarked summit.

Continue on this track and exit the west side of the woods. Walk west for a short distance, then take a left turn to descend south. At the bottom of the hill, turn left to a bridge over the railway. Once over this, follow the road south-west to the roundabout between the B4008 and A419, a short distance from the start.

Distance:	3.5 km/2 miles
Height to Climb:	120m/400ft
Start:	SO 813047
Difficulty:	2

Summit of Doverow Hill

Crawley Hill - Hetty Pegler's Tump

The summit, sometimes known as Uley Long Barrow, is a partially reconstructed Neolithic chambered mound.

About Crawley Hill

Crawley Hill is the highest point between Dursley and Stroud.

Height	251m/824ft
Summit GR:	SO 790000
Map:	O/S Explorer 168
Hill Category:	Tump

Walk Description

Whilst this hill can be added to the circuit of Cam Long Down and Downham Hill, this involves walking next to a busy road, or a short but steep unpathed ascent from the Cotswold Way. I have therefore featured it separately on this page. Follow the B4066 north from Uley. After driving for just over one mile, Crawley Hill stands 200 metres west of the road. There is a sign denoting the spot and parking available in a lay-by opposite. It is then a short walk through the field to the summit and stone chamber, see below.

Stone chamber on Crawley Hill

The Cotswolds

Summit area of Cam Long Down

The Dursley Circuit

This is a classic walk over three summits north of Dursley.

About Cam Peak

Cam Peak is an attractive grass and bracken rounded hill.

Height	184m/602ft
Summit GR:	ST 768992
Map:	O/S Explorer 167
Hill Category:	Tump

About Cam Long Down

Cam Long Down is over 100ft higher than neighbouring Cam Peak with an excellent ridge walk to reach the summit.

Height	220m/722ft
Summit GR:	ST 776995
Map:	O/S Explorer 167
Hill Category:	Tump

About Downham Hill

Downham Hill is a rounded hill on access land near the market town of Dursley.

Height	199m/653ft
Summit GR:	ST 777985
Map:	O/S Explorer 167
Hill Category:	Tump

Walk Summary

This walk starts and finishes at the car park below Cam Peak. The walk starts by climbing Cam Peak, then heads to Cam Long Down. From there it follows the Cotswold Way to the road (B4066) just north of Uley Bury. At this point it is possible to add Crawley Hill, but it is assumed this will be completed separately. The return route goes over Downham Hill, then returns to the car park by following the track which goes between Cam Peak and Cam Long Down.

Distance:	7 km/4 miles
Height to Climb:	350m/1,100ft
Start:	ST 768994
Difficulty:	3

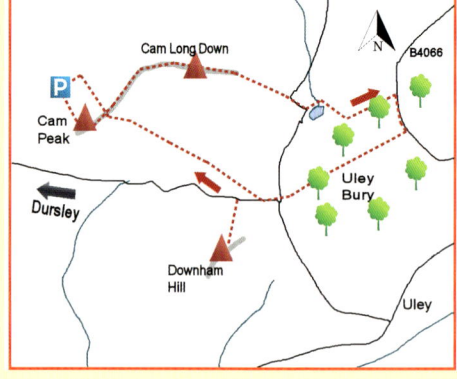

The Cotswolds

Walk Description

Summit area of Downham Hill

The walk starts from the car park just north of Cam Peak. From here it is a short climb on a grassy path between the bracken to the top of Cam Peak.

Turn left at the summit of Cam Peak and follow a good path down the east ridge. At the low point between Cam Peak and Cam Long Down, the path joins the Cotswold Way. The Cotswold Way is followed north-east then east along the attractive summit ridge of Cam Long Down. Carry on south-east following the Cotswold Way as it descends to a minor road. After following the road for a short distance, turn left to follow the Cotswold Way past Hodgecombe Farm. The path now climbs east through woods towards the B4066.

Just before reaching the road, the Cotswold Way bends left to continue north through woods. [At this point Crawley Hill can be added by staying on the Cotswold Way as it heads north through trees. After 800 metres, the path passes a forked tree. At this tree, turn right to climb steeply through the woods for 100m to the top of Crawley Hill. This climb is steep and pathless. An alternative is to continue on the Cotswold Way for another 800m to the B4066, then double back along the busy road for 400m, before turning right to Crawley Hill].

To carry on to Downham Hill, leave the Cotswold Way and continue for a short distance towards the road (B4066). Just before reaching the road turn right and then follow the right-hand path along the west edge of Uley Bury. Uley Bury is an impressive Iron Age hill fort dating back to 300 BC, standing 230m (750ft) above sea level. After 500m, a path descends right to a road T junction just below Downham Hill.

Follow the minor road west for 150m, then a concessionary path branches off to the left and climbs Downham Hill. Return to the road and walk 50m east. At the opposite side of the road from the concessionary path, a track goes north-west then west to the col between Cam Peak and Cam Long Down.

Descend directly to the car park.

The Cotswolds

The car park from Cam Peak

Stinchcombe Hill

An enjoyable circular walk round the perimeter of the golf course with excellent views over the River Severn.

About Stinchcombe Hill

Stinchcombe Hill lies above Dursley and close to the M5

Height	219m/718ft
Summit GR:	ST 737982
Map:	O/S Explorer 167
Hill Category:	Tump

Stinchcombe

Stinchcome is a small village directly below the west side of the hill it is named after.

The novelist Evelyn Waugh lived at Piers Court in Stinchcombe from 1937 to 1956 during which time he wrote Brideshead Revisited and Men at Arms.

Walk Description

From Dursley take the minor road to Stinchcombe Golf Club (put the name of the golf club in the sat-nav). Drive past the golf club car park on the right and park in the car park on the left 300m further north.

This car park adjoins the Cotswold Way. Follow the Cotswold Way west with the golf course on your right. After 1km the Cotswold Way arrives at Drakestone Point, a fine viewpoint over the Severn Valley. Now turn north and the summit Trig Point and viewfinder appears.

Continue north from the Trig Point with the golf course on your right. The Cotswolds Way bends north-east then east still following the edge of the golf course. When a minor road is reached, this can be followed south back to the car park

Distance:	3km/1.8 miles
Height to Climb:	30m/100ft
Start:	ST 744984
Difficulty:	2

Stinchcombe Hill from Drakestone Point

The Cotswolds

Bishops Cleeve from Cleeve Common

Various Hill Lists

Hill lists have evolved over the years. The best-known hill list in Britain is the Munros, the mountains in Scotland over 3,000ft, of which there were 282 at the last count. Sir Hugh Munro did not define a drop or prominence for each mountain, although it has subsequently been agreed that every mountain over 3,000ft in Scotland with a drop of 500ft on all sides should be included in the list. More recently the Wainwrights, named after Alfred Wainwright who wrote the 'Pictorial Guide to the Lakeland Fells', have become well known and the main hill list in the Lake District. There are 214 Wainwrights.

Some of the more recent hill lists have a defined drop on all sides. The best known of these is the Marilyns, a listing of all 1,556 hills in Britain with a 150m drop on all sides. Only eleven people have completed all these hills. This was followed by the HUMPs, a listing of 2,982 hills in Britain with a 100m drop on all sides. These include the famous sea stack off Orkney 'The Old Man of Hoy'. Only two people have climbed all these hills.

Finally, the TUMPs, all hills in Britain with over 30m drop, were listed. There are over 17,000 of these hills and nobody has completed them.

All the hills in the attached list are TUMPs. Sixteen are also HUMPs and six are also Marilyns. The Marilyns are the Worcestershire Beacon, Cleeve Hill, Walton Hill, Bredon Hill, May Hill, and Ruardean Hill.

The concept of Relative Hills allows hills under 2,000ft to be included in lists. In my view all the hills in this list are worth climbing, they are good hills and most have historical interest. The best-known hills in the area are the Worcestershire Beacon, Bredon Hill, and Cleeve Hill, but these don't even scratch the surface of the many fine hills dotted around the Severn Valley. Hidden gems like Cam Long Down, May Hill, Abberley Hill, Buck Stone and many more are found in this area.

The Relative Hills Society

The Relative Hills Society is a friendly, informal group, aimed at helping people meet their climbing and walking ambitions, and have fun in the hills. It aims to promote an interest in climbing British hills that are prominent relative to their surroundings including the Marilyns, Humps, Tumps and Significant Islands of Britain (SIBs) hill lists. Some of its members are active in international hill bagging which also features in the Journal.

You can find out more and join the society by visiting the Relative Hills Society website at rhsoc.uk.

by Barry Smith

On the slopes of Bredon Hill

The Various Hill Walking Lists - Explained

Hill walking lists in this book. All the hills in this book qualify as Tumps. Some are also Marilyns or Humps. All have a prominence of at least 30 metres (just under 100ft) on all sides. The heights of all these hills have been properly measured and included on the hill bagging website.

Marilyns – These are defined as having a prominence of 150 metres (nearly 500ft) on all sides. There are 174 of these in England including the 6 in this book. They are set out in the English Marilyn app which can be downloaded free from the app store.

Humps – These are defined as having a prominence of 100 metres (about 330ft). There are 444 of these in England including the 16 in this book.

Tumps – These are defined as having a prominence of 30 metres (just under 100ft). There are 3,757 Tumps in England including the 60 in this book.

There are also a number of local lists in England including the Wainwrights, Birketts and Synges in the Lake District, the Dales 30 in Yorkshire and the Ethels and Peak 75 in the Peak District.

Hills of the Severn Valley

	Hill	Area	Height (m)	Height (ft)	Prominence (m)
1	Worcestershire Beacon	The Malverns	425	1,394	337
2	North Hill	The Malverns	397	1,302	60
3	Pinnacle Hill	The Malverns	357	1,117	92
4	Herefordshire Beacon	The Malverns	338	1,109	101
5	Cleeve Hill	Cotswolds	330	1,083	234
6	Seven Wells Hill	Cotswolds	319	1,047	121
7	Walton Hill	Worcestershire	316	1,037	210
8	Four Stones Hill	Worcestershire	309	1,014	53
9	Shenbarrow Hill	Cotswolds	304	997	52
10	Birdlip Hill	Cotswolds	300	983	117
11	Bredon Hill	Worcestershire	299	981	255
12	Beacon Hill	Worcestershire	298	978	75
13	May Hill	Forest of Dean	296	972	217
14	Leckhampton Hill	Cotswolds	293	961	69
15	Ruardean Hill	Forest of Dean	290	951	174
16	Chapman's Hill	Worcestershire	287	942	55
17	Midsummer Hill	The Malverns	284	932	80
18	Abberley Hill	Worcestershire	283	928	145
19	Painswick Beacon	Cotswolds	283	928	76
20	Edge Hill	Forest of Dean	281	920	47
21	Buck Stone	Forest of Dean	280	917	146
22	Wigpool Common	Forest of Dean	279	915	39
23	Woodbury Hill	Worcestershire	275	904	90
24	Crickley Hill	Cotswolds	273	896	41
25	Swinyard Hill	The Malverns	272	892	30
26	Rednall Hill	Worcestershire	268	879	47
27	Walsgrove Hill	Worcestershire	265	869	56
28	Frankley Beeches	Worcestershire	256	840	32
29	Ragged Stone Hill	The Malverns	254	833	95
30	Crawley Hill	Cotswolds	251	824	98

Log of Walks

Date Climbed	Companions	Weather	Other Details

Hills of the Severn Valley

	Hill	Area	Height (m)	Height (ft)	Prominence (m)
31	Blakes Wood	Forest of Dean	243	797	33
32	Swell Hill	Cotswolds	235	771	38
33	Staple Edge Hill	Forest of Dean	228	748	61
34	Little Doward	Forest of Dean	222	730	128
35	Cam Long Down	Cotswolds	220	722	92
36	Stinchcombe Hill	Cotswolds	219	718	48
37	Blaze Bailey	Forest of Dean	208	682	62
38	Minchinhampton Common	Cotswolds	207	679	32
39	Serridge Inclosure	Forest of Dean	207	679	33
40	Chase Wood Hill	Forest of Dean	203	666	127
41	Crabtree Hill	Forest of Dean	203	666	35
42	Huntley Hill	Forest of Dean	202	663	54
43	Coppet Hill	Forest of Dean	201	659	140
44	Downham Hill	Cotswolds	199	653	58
45	Robins Wood Hill	Forest of Dean	198	650	142
46	Chestnuts Hill	Forest of Dean	196	643	50
47	Chase End Hill	The Malverns	191	627	58
48	Rodge Hill	Worcestershire	188	617	39
49	Cam Peak	Cotswolds	184	602	30
50	Howlers Heath	The Malverns	182	597	60
51	Hangman's Hill	Forest of Dean	180	591	32
52	Suckley Hills	The Malverns	170	558	81
53	Suckley Hills -West Top	The Malverns	164	537	36
54	Churchdown Hill	Forest of Dean	155	509	104
55	Ankerdine Hill	Worcestershire	149	489	41
56	Doverow Hill	Cotswolds	143	469	31
57	Piper's Hill	Worcestershire	120	393	31
58	Nut Hill	Cotswolds	119	390	35
59	Elbury Hill	Worcestershire	98	320	54
60	Sandhurst Hill	Forest of Dean	88	288	70

Log of Walks

Date Climbed	Companions	Weather	Other Details

Notes